UNDERSTANDING SCIENCE LESSONS

FIVE YEARS OF SCIENCE TEACHING

Michael J. Reiss

Open University Press
Buckingham · Philadelphia

To John Gray and Jean Rudduck

the autobiography of the researcher is always present
(Lea and West, 1995: 178)

Open University Press
Celtic Court
22 Ballmoor
Buckingham
MK18 1XW

email: enquiries@openup.co.uk
world wide web: www.openup.co.uk

and
325 Chestnut Street
Philadelphia, PA 19106, USA

First Published 2000

A catalogue record of this book is available from the British Library

ISBN   0 335 19769 8 (pb)   0 335 19770 1 (hb)

Library of Congress Cataloging-in-Publication Data
Reiss, Michael J. (Michael Jonathan), 1958-
    Understanding science lessons: a longitudinal study/Michael J. Reiss.
        p. cm.
    Includes bibliographical references and index.
    ISBN 0-335-19769-8 (pbk.) – ISBN 0-335-19770-1 (hc)
        1. Science–Study and teaching. I. Title.
    Q181 .R44 2000
    507'.1'242–dc21   99-044088

Typeset by Type Study, Scarborough
Printed in Great Britain by St Edmundsbury Press Ltd, Bury St Edmunds, Suffolk

Contents

Acknowledgements

My biggest thank you, of course, goes to the pupils, their parents and the staff who allowed me to conduct this study. Without you it simply would not have been possible. You have been wonderfully helpful.

I am particularly grateful to Homerton College, Cambridge, who funded the travel for all my journeys to the school and to pupils' homes and who lightened my teaching load throughout the study, enabling me to spend more time on research.

I am also very grateful to my Open University Press editor, Shona Mullen, and her assistant, Anita West, who patiently allowed me to keep on delaying my deadline for submission yet retained (I think) some belief in the worth of what I was doing.

I benefited from valuable insights from a range of colleagues, especially when preliminary versions of some of the findings were presented at seminars at Pasmoor School (1997), one of the Nuffield 'Beyond 2000' weekends (1997), Homerton College (1999), and at conferences for the Association for Science Education Tutors (1995 and 1996) and the European Science Education Research Association (1997 and 1999). Finally, Jenny Chapman very kindly read through the entire draft manuscript and made many improvements.

1

Children learning science

... consistency in theory is proof merely of disregard for the facts
(Suttie [1935]1988: 243)

8 September, 8.45 a.m.

It is 8.45 a.m. and I am waiting at the back of a secondary school science laboratory. In most respects it is just like the one in which I first learnt science. There are large benches, rather than individual desks, and these have supplies of water, electricity and gas. Round the outside of the room there are cupboards with familiar scientific apparatus – Bunsen burners, tripods, test-tube racks and so on.

As I sit, somewhat nervously, in the corner of the room, the teacher, Stephen Benton, lets the pupils in. They stream in and, remarkably quickly it seems to me, choose places to sit. My first, somewhat irrational, thought is that except for the fact that some are girls and some are boys, the pupils all look remarkably alike.

Today, 8 September, is these pupils' first science lesson (a double period) since arriving at Pasmoor School. All of them are 11 years old and they have come from a wide variety of primary schools and family backgrounds.

Stephen spends quite a few minutes at the beginning of the lesson sorting out names – who is present and on the list of names he has that details who is expected, who is present but not on his list, and who is on his list but not present. Four of the pupils in the room are not on Stephen's list and he gently sends them off to other rooms. He then checks whether each of the remaining pupils likes certain abbreviations for their first names and goes through their science timetables with them, ensuring they know when the lessons are.

At this point one of the four pupils Stephen had sent away – Liz – returns. It turns out that she is meant to be in this group, but is just here for a year and then will return to her home country overseas.

In all, there are just 19 pupils – I had expected more. Seven of them are girls and 12 are boys. There are three long benches in the room, each with its longer axis facing the teacher. At the front of the room, at right angles to these three benches, there is the teacher's bench. Behind it and to one side is a science prep room. The girls have all sat at the bench nearest the door. The boys are split equally between the other two pupil benches.

Stephen explains to the class that science classes are smaller than their tutor groups and that it looks like they'll be in this lab for the whole year, though sometimes some science lessons are done in ordinary classrooms rather than in labs.

At 9.04 a.m., having sorted all that out, Stephen welcomes them and says that science is fun, but that it has to be safe. He gets pupils to say whether or not they have done any science and to say what science is. Stephen starts with the girls and is careful to involve pupils from all three benches.

At 9.08 a.m. Stephen talks positively about how much science they seem to have done: more than in previous years, he says, mentioning that nobody, before this year, has ever talked about doing chemistry before. Stephen then tells them that their first topic, which will last until half-term is called 'Being a scientist', then they will go on to do 'Materials', then 'Energy' (including light and sound), then 'Bodies' (including cells and reproduction), then 'Reactions', then 'Forces' and finally – the last topic of Year 7 – 'The environment' which will include surveys and animal behaviour.

At 9.12 a.m. Stephen asks them 'What is science?' He gets three answers: 'Finding things out', 'Doing experiments' and 'Fairness'. Throughout the lesson Stephen reacts positively to any answers, encouraging the pupils by saying 'That's right' or, when the answer is less appropriate, words to the effect of 'To some extent'. Stephen then asks them what they need to do before doing an experiment. It soon becomes clear to me that he is thinking of 'Planning', though the answers he gets are 'Gather materials', 'Protective things' and 'Make sure you're not going to make something dangerous'.

Stephen asks them what scientists have found out about. 'Curing cancer' and 'Space' he is told. Stephen explains how the science that went into the Americans sending someone to the Moon is now used for clothing, etc.

Stephen asks them to name some scientists. 'Einstein' is the first suggestion, then 'Isaac Newton'. Stephen asks them for some female scientists, but no one can name one, so he tells them a bit about Marie Curie, and then about Helen Sharman. Stephen says that one of them might be an important scientist in the future.

At 9.18 a.m. I write in my notebook: 'I've enjoyed the 1st half hour – feels positive for pupils, if perhaps some fidgeting a bit'. At this point Stephen gives each pupil an exercise book and at 9.24 a.m. he hands out a list of 11 science rules and goes through them with the class. Rule number four states: 'When instructed to use a Bunsen burner, make sure that hair, scarves, ties, etc. are tied back or tucked in to keep them well away from the flames' and Stephen tells them that over the years he only remembers two or three pupils whose hair caught alight, a remark which makes an impression on some of the pupils.

Stephen carefully explains the reasons for the rules. For example, the reason for 'not eating' – unless, very occasionally, he tells them to – is because the food might have got some dangerous chemicals on it. Stephen then goes on to explain about what the procedure would be if this did happen: they would have to have their mouth washed out or even be hosed down. Stephen tells them that science labs are actually one of the safest places in schools.

Stephen asks them what 'flammable' might mean. He encourages them to think what it sounds like. He gets Jane – who hasn't put her hand up – to answer.

During all this I'm scribbling furiously. My first impressions of individuals who stand out are of Liz who seems quite outgoing – she asks what 'Tipp-Ex' means when Stephen uses the word – and of George who tells a story about someone's hair catching alight because of meths at a barbecue. The fire got put out, George says, by someone 'scrunching' her hair. Stephen says that that was a very good idea because it got rid of the oxygen.

At 9.44 a.m. Stephen sets them their homework: to stick the lab safety rules into their exercise books and get their parents/guardians to sign that they have read the rules with their child. In answer to a question Stephen explains that wearing a CDT (craft, design and technology) apron or old shirt is optional – he doesn't insist on it.

At 9.50 a.m. Stephen hands out a worksheet titled 'Rainbow fizz'. This is all about carrying out a series of chemical reactions by carefully pouring the contents of test-tubes into other test-tubes and observing the results. The worksheet says that they should 'Observe using all your senses' and Stephen gets them to say what the senses are. He says that it's OK to touch around the tube to see if it gets hot, but that they mustn't taste. He explains about how to smell carefully. George volunteers the information that he thinks he may have done this with his science kit at home. Stephen says 'Good' and explains that that's good because it's quite difficult to do all the observations at one go.

At 9.55 a.m. Stephen carefully goes through the instructions, emphasizing that the liquids must be added very slowly. At 10.00 a.m. the pupils start doing the experiment. They stand up, follow the instructions, talk among themselves about what they are doing and begin to make their observations and record their results. At 10.10 a.m. I note that everyone seems to be enjoying the experiment. One group seems to me to be working a bit too quickly, but even they end up getting quite good results. All in all, the pupils spend 25 minutes carrying out the experiment and recording their results.

The double lesson is scheduled to end at 10.25 a.m. At about that time Stephen says he will keep the final tubes to show his Year 11 class, to get them to work out what is going on. Stephen then gets the class to clear up and at 10.29 he compliments them on their work and dismisses them.

Over the next five years I came to know these pupils well as I carried out a longitudinal study of their learning in science lessons.

The aims of the study

My original research background was in animal behaviour. I spent a certain amount of time on the Island of Rhum, off the west coast of Scotland. Here I would sit, four hours at a time, with a pair of excellent binoculars, watching the red deer on the island and recording aspects of their behaviour. The academic study of animal behaviour became transformed some 40 years ago by the pioneering work of Jane Goodall who went in 1960 to study the chimpanzees at the Gombe reserve on the banks of Lake Tanganyika.

The crucial thing about Goodall's research was that she concentrated on the natural behaviour of individual chimpanzees over a period of many years. In this sense her research is like the ethnographic work carried out by anthropologists when they study individuals and groups of people in a culture over an extended period of time. Goodall's accounts of the activities of such individuals as Flo and Figan are memorable and have transformed our understanding of how animals behave in the wild (Goodall 1986).

However, when I read papers or books on science education, I very rarely read much that is memorable about individual children. It is not, of course, that ethnographic research is rare in schools; far from it. Rather, it is that it almost never seems to be used in science lessons over long periods of time. Two notable exceptions are the work of Bonnie Shapiro and Gustav Helldén.

Bonnie Shapiro has spent over a decade examining in detail what one group of schoolchildren understand about the physics of light (Shapiro 1994). By now her original pupils have long left school. However, she succeeds in keeping in touch with most of them, still talking with them about their understanding of light. Indeed, she and I have even talked together about the possibility of hiring private detectives to try to find the occasional individuals who almost inevitably become 'lost' from longitudinal studies over the course of the years.

Shapiro's work demonstrates the huge differences there are between what different children know about a science topic. Of especial importance, she manages to relate what individual pupils know to their personal characteristics – whether, for example, they are fascinated or bored by science, whether they think about science out of school and whether they are good observers or not.

Gustav Helldén too has spent over a decade studying one group of pupils. He has focused on their understanding of biological processes, interviewing the same individuals on various occasions between the ages of 9 and 15 (Helldén, 1998a, 1998b, 1999). One of his more depressing conclusions is that the actual school science teaching the pupils received had very little influence on their ideas.

On moving to a post in science education at Homerton College, Cambridge, I decided to start a piece of research involving fieldwork. I intended to follow a group of children through a number of their science lessons over a period of at least two years. In the event I studied them for five, remaining with them from their first lesson as 11-year-olds at the beginning of Year 7 in September

1994 to their last lessons as 16-year-olds at the end of Year 11 in May 1999. My hope was that the findings might shed light on two main questions:

- How do pupils experience school science lessons?
- Why do some pupils enjoy science and do well in it, while others don't?

How I carried out the work

Choice of school

The school in which I worked was identified by me because it satisfied the following criteria:

- The school needed to be a state (i.e. non-fee paying) school with a non-selective intake of both girls and boys.
- Science should be taught in mixed-ability classes for at least the first year.
- The school should be reasonably near to Cambridge (for my ease of travel).
- The school and its science department should be considered to be good ones. I wasn't interested in finding out that many pupils failed to enjoy science or did poorly in it simply because the school or the science department were poor.
- The science department should not be one where I had previously had a student doing their teaching practice. In other words, the members of the science department should not already know me well. This criterion was chosen because I didn't want a science department which might already know my views on what constituted 'good science lessons'.

Only a small minority of schools fulfilled these criteria. The hardest criterion to fulfil was the last one. I had spent the previous six years on a series of short-term contracts as a lecturer in science education at the University of Cambridge Department of Education – only a mile from Homerton College, Cambridge. The bulk of my work there entailed running a succession of one-year teacher training courses for graduates who were learning to become science teachers. This meant that I had had students doing their teaching practice in most good science departments nearby. Thankfully, the head of science and headteacher of the first school I approached which met all the criteria for this study agreed to let me work there and it was agreed that I could start watching the lessons of one of the Year 7 science sets.

Information on the examination performance and pupil attendance at this school, which I call Pasmoor School, is given for 1994 (the year I began the study) and 1997 (the year the pupils began their GCSEs) in Table 1.1. Throughout the study, the school ranked near the top of the non-selective state schools in the local education authority on the criterion of the percentage of pupils gaining five or more GCSEs at grades A* to C. In other words, on these admittedly rather narrow criteria, the school was an academically

Table 1.1   Examination performance at GCSE (General Certificate of Secondary Education, the examinations taken by the great majority of pupils in England and Wales when aged 16 years) and school attendance for Pasmoor School in 1994 and 1997 compared with the whole of England

1994

	GCSEs (%)			% of half days missed due to absence	
	5+ A^*–C	5+ A^*–G	1+ A^*–G	Authorized	Unauthorized
Pasmoor School	63	99	100	6.5	0.1
England average	43.3	85.6	92.3	7.8	0.9

1997

	GCSEs (%)			% of half days missed due to absence	
	5+ A^*–C	5+ A^*–G	1+ A^*–G	Authorized	Unauthorized
Pasmoor School	73	98	98	6.3	<0.05
England average	45.1	86.4	92.3	7.9	1.0

successful one. In addition, I understood from friends with children there and from colleagues that both the school and the science department seemed to enjoy a good reputation.

Classroom observations

In the manner beloved by ethnographers researching in schools, I collected a certain amount of data while observing pupils in corridors and in the school grounds between lessons. I also analysed pupil exercise books and made observations on such occasions as staff meetings, parents' evenings and the opening of new science laboratories at the school. However, the great bulk of my data were obtained during lessons or interviews.

Classroom observations were recorded as I sat quietly in the back of science lessons making notes in a field notebook. In all, I sat in on 563 50-minute lessons, most of which were double periods, i.e. 100 minutes of continuous science. This represents approximately 60 per cent of the maximum number of lessons I could have seen (see Table 1.2). In fact, only two pupils I studied had the opportunity to go to the 1008 lessons recorded in Table 1.2. This was because only these two pupils out of my original group chose during Years 10 and 11 to study 'Triple Award' science, leading to three GCSEs. The great majority of pupils in the school as a whole and in the group I was following studied 'Double Award' science, leading to two GCSEs. These pupils could have attended a maximum of 818 lessons. Given an average absence rate of 6.4 per cent (see Table 1.1), a typical pupil would have therefore gone to a total of round about 766 50-minute science lessons during their five years at the school.

Table 1.2   The number of science lessons at the school and the number I observed in each year of the study

Year	Number of science lessons	Number I observed	%
Year 7	147	88	60
Year 8	150	87	58
Year 9	141	102	72
Year 10	317	160	50
Year 11	253	126	50
Total	1008	563	56

The chance of my getting to a particular science lesson was determined entirely by whether or not I had other commitments, such as my own teaching. In the first year of the study I always told the teacher in advance if I would not be able to get to his next lesson. In subsequent years I gave the deputy head of science before the start of each term a list of times I could manage to get to the school. She very kindly then prepared a rota for me and distributed copies of this among the teachers whose classes I was observing. She did her best to ensure that I managed as even a spread of lessons across the different groups as was possible. Throughout the study all teachers, learning support assistants and student teachers allowed me to watch their lessons.

During the lessons I functioned almost entirely as a non-participant observer, taking detailed notes (about 600 words a lesson). The skill here is to be unobtrusive and, indeed, appear fairly unobservant. I believe, in a manner some might consider archetypal of male teachers, I managed to wear the same jacket on every visit I made to the school. More importantly, I chose to remain seated at the back of the room for the duration of each lesson. This had the obvious disadvantage that when the pupils were working individually or in small groups, I was much more likely to see and hear only what those near to me were doing.

However, sitting quietly at the back had a major advantage in that I believe I had comparatively little effect on what went on in the lessons. Pupils, in particular, came to regard me as 'part of the furniture'. Indeed, I was encouraged by the surprise shown, in later years of the study, by new teachers to the school who commented, on a number of occasions, on how the pupils seemed to pay no attention to me.

This is not to claim that I was invisible nor that I had no effect on what went on in lessons. Ever since the work of Heisenberg in formulating his uncertainty principle we have become used to the notion that even in physics experiments the observer affects that which is observed. And what is true for physics experiments is far more true when it comes to humans watching humans. An unusually dramatic illustration of this in educational research is given by the following quote:

> the researcher who was in her second year of observing classrooms . . . got talking to a student on the way to school. 'We like Thursdays because it is the day you come'. 'Why should that be?' asked the researcher. 'Because', said the student, 'we don't get hit on Thursdays'.
> (MacBeath *et al.* 1996: 11)

Whether I had quite this effect on what went on in the lessons I observed I doubt, though, strictly, I cannot know for certain. To a certain extent, the very fact that I watched so many lessons reduces, I feel, the likelihood that what I saw differed importantly from what a truly invisible observer would have recorded. However, there were just a handful of occasions when I played a more active role. On one occasion I quietly but firmly stopped a pupil from doing something for reasons of safety. And on about three or four occasions over the five years a teacher left me in charge of a class for a few minutes. On one of these occasions, in the first year of the study, the teacher, after checking that I was prepared to, left me to bring the lesson to a close. I confess I quite enjoyed the surprise in many pupils' eyes at my demonstration that I knew their names and could function as a normal science teacher.

Throughout the study I tried as far as possible not to catch pupils' eyes when I was in lessons, preferring instead to keep my head down if any pupils were looking in my direction. I was especially careful to do this when listening to any pupil comments. Although this meant, on occasions, that I failed to hear some tantalizing communication, it did make it more likely that what I noted was not said or done for my benefit. When pupils asked me what I was writing down or doing I said (truthfully but rather uninformatively) that I made notes on what was going on in the lessons. I made it clear, though, that I didn't want to get into conversations during lessons. In a further effort to minimize the possibility of pupils realizing that I had heard or seen something of especial interest, I would typically wait for some 30–60 seconds after such instances before writing anything in my notes.

I did briefly wonder about whether to video some lessons. Videotaping can produce extremely rich data (Plowman 1999) and has been used with success in science lessons (e.g. Ogborn *et al.* 1996). I have used videotapes to record red deer behaviour. However, a disadvantage, for the type of work I was interested in, is that videotaping almost inevitably turns the 'subjects' – i.e. teachers and pupils – into 'actors'. Indeed, how can it not? At best, one hopes that the actors act as themselves and are good at it. But there remains the strong possibility that some of them will act what they think you want to see or what they think you don't want to see or, in the manner of certain sports spectators waving idiotically at a camera, what they would like themselves or their friends to see. In any event, actors begin their careers by acting self-consciously. As soon as we reflect consciously on our behaviour, not only does that behaviour change, but we change, with possible future consequences both for ourselves and for our observable behaviours.

Interviews

Halfway through Year 7, I wrote to the parents of all the 21 pupils in the class. (Two pupils, both boys, joined the 19 pupils in the class after the initial lesson summarized at the start of this chapter.) The letter told them a bit about myself and the focus of my research and asked them if they would kindly let me come and interview their daughter/son at home. I was extremely relieved that 19 of the 21 sets of parents agreed to this. Indeed, the other two agreed from Year 8. The initial interview halfway through Year 7 was only with the pupils. At the end of Year 7 and each subsequent year I interviewed each pupil, one or both parents and each teacher, learning support assistant and student teacher who had taught classes during the year with any of the 21 pupils I was following.

With the exception of two sets of parents and their children in Year 7 and one set of parents and their daughter in Year 10, all parents, pupils and staff at Pasmoor School agreed to be interviewed by me on every occasion I asked. (In Year 11 I chose not to approach one set of parents and only interviewed their daughter.) However, 6 of the 21 pupils left Pasmoor School before the end of Year 11. Two of these moved to nearby schools, one during Year 10, the other at the end of Year 10, and I maintained contact with them. Of the other four, two moved back to the USA towards or at the end of Year 7, one emigrated to New Zealand at the end of Year 7 and I was unable to trace the whereabouts of the fourth who left during Year 8. Letters, e-mails and a meeting when she was visiting a friend – one of the pupils in this study – enabled me to keep in touch with one of the American pupils.

All this made for a total of 225 interviews. In this total, each parental interview counts as 'one' irrespective of whether only one or both parents were present for the interview. With one exception, I never interviewed parents separately from each other. Pupils and parents were always interviewed in their homes. Teachers, learning support assistants and student teachers were mostly interviewed at Pasmoor School, though some interviews were conducted in their homes, some in my home, some in my room at work and some at the institutions where the student teachers were training. In addition, four interviews with student teachers were conducted over the telephone.

Educational research interviews are frequently, perhaps usually, audio-taped and subsequently transcribed (e.g. Cohen and Manion 1994). I decided not to do this. Instead, I made notes during the interviews and wrote up my notes within, at most, 24 hours – usually within 4 hours. A typical interview lasted for about 20 minutes and resulted in approximately 700 words of write-up.

There are several manifest disadvantages with my decision not to audiotape the interviews. For one thing, no one can check my audiotapes. Then there is the obvious fact that an interviewer can only write down a small proportion of what an interviewee says. This means that I had continuously to select what to record. In effect, I was partially analysing the data as I listened.

However, I decided not to tape-record interviews for a number of reasons. The most important stems from how I still remember the first time, some ten years ago, that I was interviewed by someone else undertaking a piece of educational research. Despite the fact that I already knew and liked the interviewer and despite the fact that he showed considerable expertise in his interviewing technique, trying to put me at ease and so forth, I felt uncomfortable during the interview. I spoke in a more stilted manner than usual and thought less before speaking than is my wont. I certainly made no off-the-cuff remarks. Now this may simply reflect certain inadequacies in my own personality! I think I, subconsciously, treated the interview as if it was an examination to a far greater extent than when people have interviewed me without using tape-recorders. As far as this study goes, I thought it possible that some of my interviewees would similarly find the presence of a tape-recorder to be strange or even inhibiting.

In the event, I soon became convinced that I had done the right thing not to use a tape-recorder. For a start, I think it likely that some of the participants would not have granted me permission to use a tape-recorder. I was extremely keen to ensure that my sample was not skewed by the omission of certain people. Then, in addition to helping subjects relax, an unexpected bonus of my writing notes during the interview was that this slowed down the proceedings. For some pupils, in particular, these pauses helped them to say more. Finally, a third advantage came from the fact that the absence of a tape-recorder blurred the boundaries of the interview. Interviewees often made some of their most interesting remarks as I met them or at the end of the formal interview.

On at least the first occasion that I interviewed each participant (child or adult), I explained about confidentiality and the use of different names if I eventually wrote up the material for publication. All interviewees gave me permission to use the material for publication and many interviewees – pupils, parents and staff – discussed with me the purpose of the research and its broad findings on more than one occasion.

All my interviews were semi-structured in the sense that I went with a prepared list of, typically, half a dozen to a dozen questions. I took particular care to ensure that none of the questions were leading ones or might have been felt as such. For example, even in the final interview with pupils at the end of Year 11, when I asked them a question about what they were going on to do now that they had left Pasmoor School, I didn't ask those who had chosen not to study science in some form why this was the case, for fear that this might have implied that I thought they should have.

Each year I prepared a new set of questions and asked different questions to the various groups – i.e. pupils, parents, teachers, learning support assistants and student teachers. Within each group – e.g. within the pupils – I asked the same questions in any one year to all group members.

I decided not to use interviews to determine pupils' knowledge about science. I had two main reasons for this. First, I didn't want the interviews to be felt to be assessment instruments. I wanted pupils to feel relaxed and unthreatened in the interviews. Second, I thought that I could probably get sufficient measures of pupils' scientific knowledge through classroom observations, backed up by their teachers' views and their own performances on homeworks, tests and public examinations.

Some recent research suggests that choosing not to use interviews to determine pupils' knowledge about science may have been the right decision. Welzel and Roth (1998) report that there are considerable problems in using interviews in this way. For a start, what individuals know varies in a variety of ways over both shorter and longer timescales. Perhaps more importantly, there are considerable interactions between the complexity of the questions asked by the interviewer and the complexity of the thinking revealed by the interviewees' responses.

These difficulties can be surmounted. But they need to be overcome in much the way that good examiners organize examination papers so that pupils are enabled to reveal what they do know in response to a question rather than what they do not know. This takes not just care but time. As will be seen in later chapters, I chose to use the interviews for other purposes.

Analysing the data

All data need analysis and analysis begins with the selection of those data which the researcher considers most relevant. Obviously a five-year study of this type generates an extremely large mass of information. I have, for example, records of all the occasions pupils left the room to go to the toilet (and am willing to consider joint analysis of these findings with any interested urologist).

My interview notes consisted mostly of verbatim quotations. When I wrote these up I also included comments about how I felt and how I thought the interviewee felt. Clearly this is extremely subjective, but the reason for my noting feelings is connected with my having been trained as a psychodynamic counsellor. It was Freud who, initially, thought that he should ignore his own feelings about clients. Soon, though, he realized that he could learn a tremendous amount by analysing why he felt about certain clients as he did – for example, why he liked some or was bored by others. In technical language, this is known as analysing the countertransference. By now, this practice is commonplace among psychoanalysts, psychotherapists and counsellors trained within a psychodynamic framework (e.g. Casement 1985; Sandler *et al.* 1992).

As far as this study goes, the important point is that I tried to reflect on why I felt as I felt. Why, for example, did I feel sympathetic towards certain pupils but occasionally irritated by others? Why was I more likely, as my initial reaction, to excuse the 'mistakes' made by certain teachers in the classroom compared with others? Often I was able to work out the answers to these questions. It would be nice if I could unfailingly partition these answers into those that were to do only with me and those that were to do only with those I was interviewing, but I doubt that I can with complete accuracy.

What I can try to do is to be clear about how I felt and why I think I felt as I did. Hopefully this will often allow you, the reader, to decide for yourself whether you agree with my interpretation or not. I must emphasize again that much of what is included in this book is a series of interpretations by me. Sometimes these will say more about me than they do about those I was observing or questioning or about the state of science education in England in the late 1990s more generally. I must, therefore, genuinely apologize for the times when I have misheard, misunderstood or misinterpreted what was going on.

Pseudonyms

Our names are important to us. Most of us keep the first name(s) our parents gave us throughout our lives. Some of us change our surnames on marriage though increasing numbers of married people retain 'their' surnames. Yet, as is standard practice when academic research is written up for publication, all names included here (except mine) are pseudonyms.

At first I drew up a list of such pseudonyms. However, during one of the Year 10 interviews, a pupil told me that he would like me to use a particular name for him. I agreed and therefore, during the Year 11 interviews with pupils and teachers, I asked them whether they too had a first name they would like me to use for them. Ten pupils and two teachers gave me such a name. (Interestingly, one pupil chose the name I had already allocated him!) These names are used in the study. (Several pupils suggested I use their real name but I explained that I wouldn't – so much for my asking them what name they would like me to use for them!) All other names are chosen by me. I soon found, though, that choosing names was more problematic than I had anticipated.

The easy thing is to ensure that the names indicate sex appropriately – though this does exclude from use that small minority of names, such as 'Sam' and 'Chris', which are indeterminate with regard to sex. But what of class and ethnicity? As far as the head of science was aware, Pasmoor School kept no records on pupils' ethnicity. It was apparent to me, though, that the percentage of both pupils and staff that would have described themselves as 'white' was considerably higher than the national figure for England of around 93 per cent. In the end, I chose names by ethnicity so as to reflect the percentage of the pupils and staff I studied who would, I felt, have described themselves as belonging to a particular ethnic group. However, I deliberately did not intend the names of individuals necessarily to reflect their ethnicity.

The connections between first names and social class in England are considerable, though sometimes subtle. Their importance was clearly indicated by one of the male teachers whom I interviewed at the end of Year 11. When asked by me whether he had a name he would like me to use for him, he said that he had no preference but then added 'I might be offended if I turned up as a Darren!' I got hold of lists of the most popular current names for children and used these and other names that occurred to me during the last two years of the study to assign names. My hope is that no one who recognizes themselves will feel unhappy with the pseudonym I gave them.

There are times, though, when pseudonyms offer inadequate protection against identification. For this reason, I have sometimes omitted even the pseudonyms when I thought their inclusion would be unhelpful for the individuals concerned. However, I have not changed any details, unlike some researchers who do this so as further to increase anonymity. Such a practice is, in my view, to blur too far the distinction between a portrayal of reality and the invention of a fiction.

Questions of objectivity and subjectivity

I have already alluded to the fact that there are times when events included here will have been inaccurately reported or interpreted by me. However, there is far more to the issue of objectivity and subjectivity than the making of the odd mistake. As the quotation included in the preliminary pages of this book indicates, there is no such thing as a purely objective account. What I write is inevitably shaped by who I am. Had others conducted the same study I am sure their accounts would have differed from mine. That much is obvious. What is, of course, not so clear, is how greatly their accounts would have differed.

In recent years, educational researchers have increasingly, and in my view healthily, grown suspicious of those within their ranks who present a single description of events (Rhedding-Jones 1997). We now doubt those who purport to be able to provide a single canonical version of past events. After all, as has been widely noted, history is too often 'his story' – i.e. a story told by just one person from one particular perspective. Unreflective perspectives tend, often without intending so, to marginalize or misrepresent those who have different perspectives.

Surely it is better for me to write, instead, what I explicitly acknowledge is just one vision and interpretation of events. Whether any of the characters in this story will ever write their own autobiographical accounts of this period of their lives I don't know, but I would be so pleased if they did. Then others could compare the various versions, rather as theologians look at the four gospels, attempting to extract further meanings from both the agreements and the differences in the separate accounts (e.g. Davies 1967; Hayes and Holladay 1982).

Another issue to do with objectivity derives from the fact that while few of those discussed here knew anything about me at the start of the study, as time went on they and I inevitably started to develop some sort of relationship. In some cases the relationship was rather a thin one. A few parents and pupils were not that keen on my pestering them each year for yet another interview. Most parents and pupils, though, not only generously welcomed me into their homes but appreciated someone taking a genuine interest in them over a number of years. And I do mean a genuine interest. I am interested in knowing about people's lives and greatly enjoyed, in particular, the interviews I conducted with pupils, parents and staff.

By the end of the five years I felt close to quite a number of those I had come to know through the study. In a few cases it was clear that the people concerned found talking to me to be of actual therapeutic value. While I never intended the interviews to develop into counselling sessions, in a few cases interviews were conducted in harrowing personal circumstances for the individual concerned. But then, most of us value someone taking an interest in us over several years, even when things are going well.

My relationship with the school developed too. I joined the Gender Working Party. The science department generously insisted I came to one of its member's fiftieth birthday celebrations. And the school kindly invited me to the staff breakfast party on the day during the summer holidays when the GCSE results came out for the pupils I was following.

Unsurprisingly, too, given how many of their lessons I had seen, I ended up writing job references for more than one of the teachers. Some of them sent me Christmas cards and I even ended up conducting the weddings for the daughters of two of the teachers in my capacity as a priest in the Church of England. To be honest, though, that was due to accidents of geography rather than to the effect of the study itself.

Writing up the study

After toying with various possibilities, I decided to write the bulk of the study up chronologically. For this reason the next five chapters deal, respectively, with Year 7, Year 8, Year 9, Year 10 and Year 11. The final chapter attempts to draw together the various threads of the research. A different possibility would have been to have tackled in separate chapters such major themes as classroom teaching, pupil differences and parental influences, each chapter using material from several years.

I decided on the chronological approach for a number of reasons. For one thing, the study was obviously carried out chronologically rather than by themes. I didn't spend six months studying classroom teaching, followed by six months on pupil differences, etc. For that reason, a chronological account is more authentic. A second reason is that a chronological account allows me more easily to describe not only how the pupils changed over the years but how what I was interested in and what I noticed during the research did too. A final reason is that I hope a chronological account is more readable and gives a richer impression of what life in science lessons was like for pupils during the time of the study.

Obviously I have had to be selective. As the title of the book is meant to hint, I have tried to concentrate on two interrelated issues. First, on analysing and describing what pupils understood from their science lessons – that is, what they learnt of science and about science. Second, on analysing and describing what I, the researcher, understood from the study – that is, what I felt led to pupils learning what they learnt of and about science.

Key points

- There have been few longitudinal studies in science education, in which a group of children is followed over a number of years.
- Longitudinal studies can tell us a great deal about what children learn in science lessons and how they experience their science education.
- The data in this five-year longitudinal study mainly come from observations of science lessons and from interviews. One group of 21 children was followed through their 11–16 science education.
- In all, 563 50-minute science lessons were observed and 225 interviews conducted with pupils, parents and teachers.
- A study such as this cannot be fully objective. For various reasons, the observations made and conclusions reached by another researcher would have differed from mine in at least some respects.

2

Year 7: New children, new school

If they come with nothing, they'll see nothing. They have to come
with something.

(Jarman 1988)

The world of science

All the pupils in this research had studied science in their previous schools
before coming to Pasmoor School. Indeed, most of them arrived from English
state primary schools which had been teaching the National Curriculum since
1989. The National Curriculum (England and Wales) has probably had more
of an effect in primary schools on the teaching of science than on any other
subject. Along with English and mathematics, science has been designated
one of the three core subjects of the curriculum (Department of Education
and Science and the Welsh Office 1991). These three subjects alone are tested,
for the very great majority of pupils, towards the end of Year 2, Year 6, Year 9
and Year 11.

English and mathematics have always been taught in primary schools, as
the 'three Rs' of reading, writing and arithmetic imply. The extent of science
teaching steadily increased in primary schools during the 1970s and 1980s
thanks to the enthusiasm of primary teachers and the exhortations of Her
Majesty's Inspectorate, advisers and others in positions of influence (Osborne
and Simon 1996). However, it was the introduction of the National Curriculum that galvanized primary teachers into teaching not just more science
but a more systematic version of science, with a strong emphasis on
investigations and the inclusion of elements from a range of subjects within
science – astronomy, biology, chemistry, earth sciences and physics (Summers et al. 1993).

Despite this recent strengthening of primary science and despite the fact
that as I watched him teach it was clear that Stephen Benton often made links
between what was being done in his lessons and in (the rest of) the 'real

world', the impression I as an observer gained was that Year 7 science was expected by pupils to be significantly different from anything they had done before or come across. Research on Year 6 pupils carried out at about the time that the pupils in this study were in Year 6 has shown that they expect science in secondary schools to differ markedly from science in primary schools (Jarman 1993; Hawkey 1995).

Most Year 6 children expect secondary schools to provide distinctive equipment and other facilities for science. The Bunsen burner seems to be deeply iconic in this respect (Delamont *et al.* 1988; Jarman 1993). Indeed, Delamont and her colleagues titled their paper 'In the beginning was the Bunsen: the foundations of secondary school science' in recognition of this, while Jarman similarly titled her paper 'Real experiments with Bunsen burners: pupils' perceptions of the similarities and differences between primary science and secondary science'. Ruth Jarman writes: 'In the mind of the child, it seems, the act of lighting a bunsen burner assumes the status of a rite of passage into the realm of "real" science' (1993: 23).

There is a limited amount of evidence which suggests that Year 6 pupils may now be expecting more continuity in content between primary and secondary school science, with secondary schools providing better facilities and specialist equipment – the Bunsen burner again (Campbell 1999).

My observations led me to conclude that the Year 7 science scheme of work taught by Stephen Benton – which had far more similarities to than differences from the Year 7 schemes of work I have seen in many other schools – tried to convey two messages to pupils. First that science has many connections with the rest of their lives and in that sense is relevant, real and important. And second that it is a distinctive discipline – into which they needed to be initiated – defined by its content, by its process and by its language.

The content of science

Within 20 minutes of the start of his first lesson with the new Year 7 pupils, as mentioned in Chapter 1, Stephen Benton had mapped out the content of their first year's science lessons. They would be covering seven units in all:

- Being a scientist
- Materials
- Energy
- Bodies
- Reactions
- Forces
- The environment.

This pattern was adhered to, each unit being clearly introduced as such and ending with a test. As one might expect, this content mapped tightly onto the requirements of the science National Curriculum. On my first interview with pupils, one of the questions I asked was 'What would you like to do in science

Table 2.1   Analysis of answers to Question 8 on first home visit: 'What would you like to do in science lessons?' Each pupil gave up to three answers. [] indicate my interpretation of what was said

Girls

Topic	Number of responses
Chemistry	2
Long-term experiments	1
Experiments	1
Reading and writing	1
Space/transcendence	1
Not the body – rockets more exciting	1
What we're doing now [human reproduction]	1

Boys

Topic	Number of responses
Chemistry/explosions	6
Experiments	3
Experiments with chemicals	1
Open-ended investigation	1
Using Bunsen burners	1
How things work	1
Where different chemicals come from	1
Rocket experiments	1
Bigger things rather than Bunsen burners, thermometers and stuff	1
Tests	1
Forces	1
Dissecting	1
Microscopes	1
Astronomy	1
Animals	1
Variety	1
Don't know	3

lessons?' A summary of the answers is given in Table 2.1. Four things are clear from Table 2.1:

- A wide range of science topics was mentioned.
- Chemistry topics are mentioned particularly often.
- The question is answered not just with respect to the content of science but also to its processes.
- There is a suggestion that girls and boys differ, on average, in their replies.

Pupils often made connections between the content of their science lessons and their out-of-school experiences. After a video on human pregnancy in the unit on bodies, George asked why you can't remember when you were in your mother's womb. Instead of answering, Stephen opened the question up for discussion. Michael suggested that it's because your brain isn't developed. Edward suggested that it might be in your unconscious mind even though you can't remember it. George then told the class about the difficulties his sister had in breathing after her birth.

One of the boys then talked about how his mother nearly died during one of her pregnancies (an ectopic pregnancy from what he said). Edward talked about smacking a newborn baby to get it breathing. Martin then asked about miscarriages and one of the boys said how his mother had had a miscarriage. This led onto another boy asking what happened to his mother who had had a baby that had died inside her. Ian then questioned whether the mother survives a Caesarean section and Catherine wanted to know why you get morning sickness. My notes record 'All questions answered very well by Stephen'.

Martin asked how Down's syndrome occurs and Mary enquired what qualifications you need to do a Caesarean section. Richard then asked a question about the development of the brain and heart. Michael announced that he was present when his baby brother was born and he saw the placenta. It was only the end of the lesson that brought this discussion to a close.

The process of science

Stephen Benton's lessons contained a large amount of practical work. Much of this, particularly early on in the year when they were doing the topic 'Being a scientist', was in the form of investigations. For example, a fortnight after the beginning of term, the group began an investigation into the effect of the weight of a load on the amount that a rubber band stretched. This was planned and carried out over three lessons – a single period followed three days later by a double.

Stephen was keen for them to predict their results in advance of carrying them out. Edward, who had obviously done this practical at his previous school, a state primary school to which several of the group had gone, stated, in reply to a question from Stephen to the whole class, that when the weights were removed the rubber band didn't quite go back to its original length.

There were seven sets of apparatus for this investigation which meant that Stephen required pupils to work in threes. As all seven girls were present, he assigned Mary to work with Robert and Jack, something that none of the three seemed comfortable with. Throughout Year 7, pupils naturally segregated by gender when it came to working in groups. Mary dealt with the situation by staring into space for much of the time, letting the two boys do 90 per cent of the practical work. When it came to the following double period, Mary succeeded in working on her own and rapidly, once she had got Sue to show her how to set up the apparatus, carried out a series of studies on her own, seeing what happened when the rubber band was twisted and when more than one rubber band was used.

The rubber band investigation was the first of many. Others that year included:

- the cleaning abilities of different washing powders;
- heat conduction in metals versus glass;
- the effects of insulation on heat loss;
- the amount of heat given off by different types of matches;
- factors affecting the height to which squash balls bounce.

The paucity of biology investigations is notable. This did not greatly surprise me. Biology investigations, unless they are to do with biochemistry, generally take longer than chemistry or physics investigations and are more difficult to carry out with large groups of pupils under school laboratory conditions. In addition, under the marking system of the 1991 science National Curriculum, it was also more difficult to score highly on biology investigations as the attainment of high levels required two or more independent variables to be controlled, something that is fairly atypical of even much research work in biology. Assessing the work of Darwin in his *The Origin of Species by Means of Natural Selection* and Mendel's life work by the criteria of AT1 (scientific investigation) of the 1991 science National Curriculum gives Mendel a Level 5 and Darwin a Level 3 (Reiss 1993a). Most of the Year 7 pupils at Pasmoor School were working at Level 5 in science.

Right from the beginning of the course, Stephen used investigations as opportunities to get pupils to plan their studies, make predictions, generate hypotheses, conduct their work safely, make careful observations, analyse results, plot findings and evaluate their work.

Sometimes discussions about their hypotheses allowed a number of the pupils to make contributions and to learn from one another. For example, in a part of a lesson explicitly dedicated to 'making hypotheses', Stephen posed the question 'Why does water from a tap flow downwards?' Sue suggested this was because of gravity; Edward that pressure from the tap pushes the water down; Marc that it's because the tap is facing downwards; and Nicky that the water wants to flow down.

The discussion then moved on to the question, introduced by Stephen, of why 'crumpling affects how quickly paper falls to the ground'. Nicky suggested that screwing the paper (i.e. into a ball) makes it heavier, and then Ian said 'I can't remember his name but heavier things don't always fall faster . . . he dropped a feather and a piece of metal and saw which fell faster'. Stephen agreed with this and then, as he quite often did, brought in some material about the history of science. He told them about Galileo dropping a feather and a cannon-ball off the Leaning Tower of Pisa. Stephen then went on to tell them about the significance of the atmosphere and Neil Armstrong's equivalent experiment on the Moon. In response, Michael said that crumpled paper has the same weight (as a flat sheet) but it's spread out less. Edward said that there is less gravity on the Moon but that the important thing about the Moon is that there is no air and that is why objects fall at the same speed.

The language of science

From the very beginning of the year, Stephen Benton introduced science as a subject in which language issues were important. At the start of their third lesson he said to the whole class, 'In science we have our own special words or jargon. It's a bit like learning a foreign language'. He then got pupils to describe their findings from the 'Rainbow fizz' experiment done in the first double lesson. Pupils used terms like 'frothy', 'transparent', 'bubbly', 'cold', 'green', 'didn't smell much' and 'warmer'. Stephen added 'hissing'.

For their homework that day Stephen gave them a list of words which they needed to learn how to spell: 'scientist', 'observing', 'classifying', 'sorting', 'predicting', 'hypothesis', 'idea', 'variable', 'fair' and 'test'. He gave them a number of suggestions as to how they might learn these spellings and told them that they would have a spelling test next lesson (after the weekend) and also later in the term. Stephen talked about how people differ in how well they can spell and that he was looking for personal bests – 'three out of ten might be very good . . . don't worry if you get low scores . . . I'm looking for improvement'.

As the first term progressed, Stephen gradually used more technical terms. On 30 September, in the context of an investigation into the cleaning abilities of various washing powders, he introduced the terms 'changed variable' (the type of washing powder), 'controlled variable' (temperature, amount of washing powder, number of stirs, etc.) and 'measured variable' (time for stain to disappear).

Such scientific language was reinforced as opportunities arose. For example, on 12 January, in an investigation into the amount of heat given off by different types of matches, Stephen first emphasized, as he often did, that their prediction should be based on a reason. He then talked about the 'type of matches' as the changed variable, 'the temperature every five seconds' as the measured variable and such things as 'angle held' and 'amount of water' as the controlled variables.

Often parts of lessons were geared towards getting pupils to use language in a scientifically acceptable way. On 19 January, after they had finished writing up the investigation into the amount of heat given off by matches, Stephen got the whole class to gather on their stools round his bench at the front. He introduced the topic of sound by asking them 'How do we make sound?' Marc volunteered 'Through our voice boxes', Ian 'Through friction' and Mary 'Through waves'. Stephen had a signal generator and used it to alter the frequency of the sound it was producing. He pointed towards a loudspeaker connected to the signal generator and asked what it was. Liz said 'It's a loudspeaker'. Stephen then put small polystyrene balls on the loudspeaker to show them moving around. He then increased the frequency of the sound and asked what he was doing. A number of pupils answered that he was making the sound 'louder'. By getting the class to look at the bouncing balls Stephen tried to get the pupils to distinguish between louder sounds and higher sounds.

Stephen then asked the class what the cone of the loudspeaker was doing. Michael said 'It's magnifying the sound'. This was evidently not the answer Stephen wanted. Someone, I didn't catch who, mentioned the word 'vibrations' and Stephen seized on this and linked it with what Mary had said earlier about waves. He then showed them how the polystyrene balls on the loudspeaker vibrated more quickly when the note of the sound was higher. Stephen then introduced the word 'pitch' and asked them which animals can hear high frequencies. Pupils responded with 'dogs', 'bats', 'cats', 'whales', 'sharks' and 'seals'.

Stephen told them how sound travels through water faster than through air and George told the whole class about a time he and his sister were at opposite ends of a swimming pool and shouting to each other underwater. At this point Stephen introduced tuning forks and, after a quick demonstration, distributed hacksaw blades, tuning forks, simple guitars made out of rubber bands, simple xylophones and a single recorder and told them to find out how to make loud noises, soft noises, high-pitched sounds and low-pitched sounds.

After 12 minutes of practical work, Stephen collected the apparatus in and got them to copy the following in their exercise books from the board:

Sound energy

Sound is made when an object vibrates.
Louder the sound, bigger the vibration.
Higher the pitch of sound, faster the vibration.
Speed of sound = $\dfrac{\text{distance}}{\text{time}}$ = $\dfrac{\text{300 metres}}{\text{1 second}}$

Speed of light
is much faster   = 300 metres per second
than speed of sound   = 300 m/s
Sound can be reflected.

Catherine and Nicky thought that the speed of sound was greater than the speed of light. Most pupils thought the opposite. Burt explained about seeing lightening before hearing thunder. As the hooter for the end of the lesson went, Michael talked about the fact that sound can bend and Stephen told the class to think about this.

Gender effects

Issues to do with gender have long been studied in science education. The initial impetus for such studies came mainly from the realization that few girls chose to study chemistry and physics, a situation which still pertains in most countries (Harding 1992; Equal Opportunities Commission and Ofsted 1996).

In Chapter 1 I noted that the teacher of the Year 7 group, Stephen Benton, evidently took care in the first lesson with the group to involve as wide a range of pupils as possible. He ensured that girls were, if anything, allowed to contribute before boys were. I was interested in seeing whether this continued throughout the year.

Were there differences between girls and boys in the frequency with which they interacted with their Year 7 science teacher?

To see whether there were differences between girls and boys in the frequency with which they interacted with Stephen Benton, I recorded in each lesson the identity of each pupil who had a 'scientifically meaningful audible interaction' with Stephen in a 'whole class setting'. By 'whole class setting' is meant that Stephen was having a discussion with the whole group in which every pupil could potentially participate, as opposed to a discussion with an individual or small group.

I focused on these whole class settings because on these occasions it was feasible for me unambiguously to identify the pupil with whom Stephen was interacting and to ascertain that the interaction was indeed scientifically meaningful. Within 'scientifically meaningful audible interaction' I include any comment or unit of conversation – whether initiated by pupil or teacher – that contained an utterance relating to science.

This definition excluded all teacher utterances to do with management, such as 'Sit down', 'Be quiet', 'That's right' and 'Please fetch me that flask'. It also excluded all affective and other non-scientific pupil questions and statements such as 'Wow', 'Sorry sir' and 'Can I go to the toilet?' It included utterances made by pupils to Stephen and utterances directed by Stephen at individual pupils, even if the pupil did not respond. For example the question 'Tell me, X, why the rubber band stretched' would be recorded as a scientifically meaningful interaction with X even if X didn't respond (though such one-sided interactions were extremely uncommon).

I then looked at the proportion of the total scientifically meaningful pupil-teacher utterances made by the girls and corrected this for the relative number of girls and boys present in the class on that day. For example, suppose a lesson contained ten scientifically meaningful pupil-teacher utterances in a whole class setting, four of which involved girls and six of which involved boys. This would mean that 40 per cent of the utterances involved girls. However, suppose there were 20 pupils present, 7 of whom were girls and 13 of whom were boys. Our null hypothesis would be that 35 per cent of the utterances (i.e. 7 out of 20) should involve girls. Accordingly, an index of girl participation in scientifically meaningful pupil-teacher utterances in a whole class setting is given, in this instance, by 40 per cent divided by 35 per cent, i.e. 1.14. Any figure greater than 1 means that girls are participating more than would be expected by chance; conversely, a figure of less than 1 means that boys are participating more than expected by chance.

The first lesson in each month of Year 7 in which I recorded six or more

Table 2.2   A measure of the participation by girls relative to boys in meaningful scientific interactions with Stephen Benton in a whole class setting throughout Year 7. The figure in brackets is the number of such utterances in the first lesson in the month that had more than six such utterances. A dash means that no lesson in the month contained six or more such utterances

Month	Index of girl participation in scientifically meaningful pupil-teacher utterances in a whole class setting
September	1.14 (10)
October	1.04 (11)
November	1.06 (6)
December	0.75 (20)
January	0.68 (20)
February	0.62 (16)
March	0.67 (10)
April	–
May	0.63 (6)
June	–
July	–

scientifically meaningful pupil-teacher utterances in a whole class setting was analysed in this way and the results are shown in Table 2.2. A dash means that in no lesson in that month did I record six or more scientifically meaningful pupil-teacher utterances in a whole class setting. The total number of scientifically meaningful pupil-teacher utterances in a whole class setting for the analysed lesson is shown in brackets.

Initially, girls contribute, if anything, more than boys. However, it seems as though participation by girls in scientifically meaningful pupil-teacher utterances in a whole class setting declines throughout the year to a point at which each girl, on average, is involved in only about two thirds of the number of interactions that each boy is. That is equivalent to saying that the typical boy has 50 per cent more such interactions. (Calculation of the Spearman rank correlation coefficient shows that we can be 99 per cent confident that this decline in girl participation over the year is significant: $r_s = -0.90$; $0.001 < p < 0.01$; two-tailed.)

Did the girls and boys make the same impact on their science teacher?

Eight weeks after he had taught his Year 7 class for the last of the 147 50-minute science lessons they had had with him that year, I did my first teacher interview with Stephen Benton. As part of the interview, I asked 'Can you tell me your impressions of some of the children in 7C [the class]?' He replied:

A range of children. People like Peter, for example, who are well meaning who I think do have problems, probably from home . . . there again
George, possibly social problems – strikes me as more able but idle. Clive,
apparently he was in trouble in some of the other groups . . . [Stephen
then said something like 'but I stopped that early on']. Rodney – there's
a character who's meant to be bright but does have a language problem.
If the whole thing was carried out in French . . . [i.e. he would be OK].
Then we go on to the middle of the road people. Paul – very quiet, lacked
confidence. Martin – took a certain pride in his work . . . very neat and
organized. Knew people from other primary schools . . . and therefore
very friendly with Peter and Marc and that affected his work habits. Marc
– he was generally quite keen . . . Who else have we got? [Pause.] Burt –
certainly able, a bit slower than some. Who else have we got? [Pause.] Of
the three girls always vying with each other Catherine, no, not her. Who
do I mean? [MJR: 'Nicky or Rebecca?' Catherine, Nicky and Rebecca
nearly always sat together.] The small one. [MJR: 'Nicky'.] Nicky always
worried about what she was. Rebecca was bright. Some jealousy between
Nicky and Catherine and Rebecca. [There was a slight pause and Stephen
was evidently trying to remember someone else's name. He said something like 'and the other girl with them'. I said 'Sue?']. Sue – always away
a lot. Then we had, what's her name; always had her head in a book?
[MJR: 'Mary']. Mary tried to do the best she could; spelling problems and
dyslexia though her mother didn't want too much made of that. And
then we had that nice American girl who's left. [MJR: 'Liz'. I wondered
whether to say 'Liz or Jane' but was fairly sure he meant Liz. Stephen said
something about being sorry to see her go and I agreed.] One or two
other lads [long pause]. [MJR: 'Jack and Ian'.] Oh yes. Could be cheeky.
Ian is quite bright.

There are a number of ways of analysing this, but from the point of view
of gender, the most obvious point to make is the much greater impression
that the boys made on Stephen than did the girls. The first eight pupils commented on are all boys and more of the girls than boys have had their names
forgotten.

How did girls and boys interact in the classroom?

At first a very strong gender segregation existed between girls and boys with
regard to where they sat, with whom they worked and with whom they
talked. However, during the first term at the school this began to change,
though there was great variation among the pupils in this regard.

At the start of the lesson on 2 December, George arrived with a complete
round of ammunition slung over his shoulder. Martin arrived and admired it.
Nicky went across and talked to Marc. At 9.03 a.m., 13 minutes after the
lesson had started, Peter arrived shepherded by a male teacher who very

quietly apologized to Stephen Benton. Before he left, this visiting teacher put his hand on Peter's shoulder and steered him into the spare chair nearest the door. It was the chair next to Jane. Jane blushed and glanced at me. Peter was very still. While all this was going on, Stephen Benton got George to put his ammunition away. At 9.05 a.m., Peter and I caught each other's eye, I smiled. His non-smiling expression didn't change. He had his right hand – the one nearer to Jane – up to his head and wasn't looking at the textbook he was meant to be sharing with her. At the start of practical work at 9.08 a.m., Jane immediately stood up and went to get a funnel. Peter got up and moved towards the table with George and other boys. Peter ended up working with Marc and Martin; Jane with Mary and Liz.

By this stage of Year 7, none of the working groups were ever mixed-sex. Later in the same lesson, at 9.25 a.m., Stephen put the sticky tape on a table with only boys working on it. The sticky tape was needed for pupils to stick the crystals they had been making into their exercise books. A few minutes later there was a certain atmosphere in the air as Mary had to go across to that table to get the sticky tape. Most of the boys on the table were very aware that she was there. George asked his neighbour – who is fluent in French – 'What's the French for "excuse me"?'

Interactions between the girls and boys gradually increased in frequency and variety as pupils of both sexes made little sorties from the gender-specific encampments in which they still, at this time, began each lesson. For example, on 5 December, while Stephen was setting up a demonstration to illustrate the collection of pure water from salt solution (by reflux), Catherine slowly meandered over to Peter and whispered something in his ear. The boys around him asked 'Is it Rebecca?' Then Nicky wandered over to Martin and whispered to him about Rebecca. Then Marc meandered over to the lab table on which all seven girls customarily sat – the 14 boys occupying the other two tables – at the same time as Rebecca went across to Martin as he was approaching the girls' table.

As time went by, the interactions between the girls and the boys continued to increase in frequency, variety and purpose. On 2 March the pupils spent almost all of the lesson working from worksheets and their textbook. At 9.11 a.m. Rebecca started to drift towards Peter, Marc and Martin but by coincidence Stephen Benton at that moment started to address the whole class, so she turned back. Ten seconds later Peter and Marc called her across and she went, followed ten seconds later by Nicky. Thirty seconds after that Rebecca returned to her place. Twenty seconds later Stephen, who was over by Catherine and Rebecca, called Nicky back to her place.

Over the next couple of minutes Rebecca once and Nicky twice went across to Marc, Peter and Martin. As Rebecca approached, Marc called out cheerfully 'Oh, oh. Here she comes again' and I heard either Peter or Marc say 'Because she fancies us'. At 9.18 a.m. Peter, Martin and Marc went across to Rebecca, Catherine and Nicky. Ten seconds later Stephen told them to go and sit down. Clive called out 'Stop kissing her' and Peter complained as he went back to his seat 'God. Some people!'

At 9.23 a.m. I heard George, Clive and Peter talking about 'slags' and Clive said that George dared him to say the word to Mr Benton. At 9.25 a.m. Rebecca went across and whispered something in Peter's ear before returning, 20 seconds later, to her place. One minute later Marc went across to Nicky, Catherine and Rebecca and there were whispers between Catherine and Nicky. Nicky said to Marc 'He made it up' and Marc went back and reported this to Peter. Later in the lesson, Rebecca went across to Peter, Marc and Martin for just five seconds. She then went back to Catherine and I heard Catherine say 'After school'. Rebecca went to Peter, Marc and Martin and I heard one of them say 'After school'. The toings and froings continued until the end of the lesson.

The movements around the lab required by practical work afforded both opportunities and excuses for physical contact. In the lesson on 13 March the practical – which was to find out the ignition temperature of a number of chemicals – began at 2.11 p.m. and a minute later Peter and Marc went and sat with Nicky, Catherine and Rebecca. Rebecca tried to grab Marc's goggles and he called out 'Mr Benton, she's raping me'. Stephen appeared not to hear.

At 2.30 p.m. Peter had his hand under running water, presumably having burnt it, though I didn't see this and he certainly didn't look as though he had been seriously hurt. Nicky was holding his sleeve and patting him on the back and Rebecca was holding his hand. This continued for some 90 seconds during which time they wrapped his hand in wet paper towels. Five minutes later Rebecca, Nicky and Peter were still playing at 'doctors and patient'. Two minutes later Stephen called out to Rebecca 'Can you not sit on the bench please?' Rebecca replied 'Sorry, but he's hurt himself'. Stephen replied 'Peter, can you get on please?' 'He's injured' Rebecca rejoined. At 2.40 p.m. Stephen asked Marc why he was sitting on the side. 'I've cut myself' Marc replied. One minute later Nicky was blindfolding Marc with a dry paper towel, while Catherine now held Peter's hand in a damp paper towel. Half a minute later Rebecca was holding Marc's head and half a minute after that she briefly massaged Peter's shoulders.

How do teachers respond to these interactions?

Often it was difficult for me to tell whether Stephen chose to ignore something said or done in the classroom or simply didn't notice it. However, whether or not they respond explicitly to what they hear or see, teachers effectively choose what to encourage, what to tolerate and what to forbid. To a large extent, they define the boundaries of acceptable behaviour and speech. This point was brought home to me early on in the study when, on 14 October during Year 7, I was talking with the first pupil to enter the classroom that day (Liz) about a party she and a friend were organizing. One of the boys who entered the room said something like 'Liz is chatting up Mr Reiss' (the precise words were indistinct). How would you respond? I chose to ignore the comment. I don't think Liz heard what was said, or if she did, she had already learnt as effectively as I have how to appear not to hear something.

My overall tentative conclusion from this section on gender is that it is all too easy for a teacher to forget to think about precisely which pupils are, in essence, controlling the lesson. It is noticeable that as Year 7 progressed the boys increasingly dominated the verbal exchanges with Stephen Benton. This was even more true of the exchanges to do with classroom management and discipline. The change from the first lesson, which was controlled with precision by Stephen, to some of the later ones where he was one controlling element among several, was striking.

Pupil differences

One of the benefits of a longitudinal study is that one gets to see how individuals change over time (Wadsworth 1991). This section presents brief portraits of the 21 pupils in the Year 7 class I was studying. These portraits are drawn using impressions gathered partly as I watched them in school but mainly from when I interviewed them and their parents on the two occasions I visited their homes during the year. My hope is that these accounts will complement the earlier part of this chapter about the pupils' Year 7 lessons and will also serve to add colour when, in subsequent chapters, I refer to pupils by name.

The interview questions are given in Tables 2.3 to 2.5. There is no significance to the order in which these pupil accounts are given (in alphabetical order of pseudonyms). Here and throughout the rest of the book I have used the term 'stepfather' to indicate those occasions when the family had told me about non-biological fathering, whether the biological father had died (rarely) or whether the parents had separated or divorced (usually). However, I do acknowledge that this term is not always ideal. In some cases, stepfathers were referred to within the family as 'fathers'. Often no label was used in my presence. I have made no attempt to distinguish between full and half siblings, simply referring to 'brothers' and 'sisters'. I use the term 'parents' to include both biological and step-parents.

Burt

Burt, his three older sisters and his parents lived in a large detached house in a village. In class I had mainly noticed that he had a good knowledge of science and behaved as most teachers like children to behave. After my first visit I found myself feeling that he had a very distinctive personality though I found it hard to say just how. In answer to my second question, he described Pasmoor School as 'frantic', a word he used several times in the interview. He then asked me, laughingly, whether I was concerned that the room might be bugged. I said cheerfully that that wouldn't worry me as nothing I was going to say to him had to be kept secret. We talked about bugging devices. He had seen one in London and had nearly bought it but had been £1 short. I asked him how much bugging devices cost and he said from £50 to £100.

Table 2.3 Questions asked by me of the Year 7 pupils during my first home interview with them, halfway through Year 7

1 Where was your previous school?
2 How are you finding Pasmoor School compared with your previous school?
3 How are you finding the different subjects?
4 What do you like doing when you're not in school?
5 What do you understand by the word 'science'?
6 What do you think scientists spend their time doing?
7 Tell me a bit about the science lessons you have had so far:
   (a) What have you been doing?
   (b) How have you found the science lessons?
8 What would you like to do in science lessons?

Table 2.4 Questions asked by me of the Year 7 pupils during my second home interview with them at the end of Year 7

1 How have you found your first year at Pasmoor School?
2 What have been the good things about Pasmoor School?
3 What have been the bad things about Pasmoor School?
4 How would you describe yourself?
5 How have you changed over the past year?
6 How have you found the science lessons so far?
7 What are you going to do this summer?
8 What are your hopes for next year?

Table 2.5 Questions asked by me of the parents of the Year 7 pupils during my first interview with them on my second home visit at the end of Year 7

1 What are your opinions of Pasmoor School so far?
2(a) How do you think [your child] is getting on?
2(b) How do you think [your child] is getting on in science?
3 How would you describe [your child]?
4 What was [your child] like when (s)he was younger?
5 What are your hopes for [your child] for the future?

Burt was happy to show me his room. He had a small bedroom and then a sort of converted area next to it under the roof. He showed me his coin collection and some Citadel models of soldiers, though he told me he collected these less now because they had got so expensive. He had some fine model planes hanging up and approximately 60–70 books including a number of children's classics (*Pooh*, all the *Narnia*, etc.). I told him I had read three of the *Narnia* books again the day before and he told me he was currently reading *Garfield* and *King Arthur's Legends*.

At the end of the interview I asked (as I do in all interviews) if there was anything Burt would like to add to what he had said. He asked me to read out the questions again. This I did and we went through two of them again. He told me about going sailing and went into great detail about a night-light he had found in his father's car which magnified up to x25,000. Subsequently, as I was talking with his mother before leaving, he fetched this night-light to show me and started taking it out of its case. However, his mother wasn't keen on this. Burt carried on. I sided with his mother and ended up seeing just a glimpse of the item in question as I left.

The second interview I did with Burt had a somewhat similar feel to it. When asked to describe himself he said 'Sarcastic . . . Tight with money' and then gave a long rambling answer without my being able to follow fully either what he was saying or why he was saying it: 'and whenever you see sort of things in the newspaper and whenever you see, oh I forgot that one [a story about a Labour person being a barrister's son] . . . When they suck up to the newspaper "She's a great animal lover and very experienced", when all they mean is washing a car . . .'

When I asked Burt's mother what her hopes were for him she replied 'Oh dear! It's obviously dangerous to hope. To put goals in their way. I think it's a balance between temperament, ability and interest, all three. [Pause.] At the moment my worry is he's such a bad speller'.

For all his undoubted ability, Burt certainly did have problems with spelling. On the end-of-unit test on 'Bodies', Burt was one of only two pupils to get 20 out of 20 (the other being Rebecca). The last question on that test was 'Describe in detail the journey of a sperm, from the time it leaves a testis until it fertilises an egg. Include the names of organs and tubes and explain their function'. Burt's answer was as follows:

> It got injected into the top of the verginer and it passes into the wome (it could meet an egg heer). Then it swimes up to the top of the wome and Then it goes into one of the flopen tubes were (it should) it meets an egg, it then eats away at the jely coat untill it gets into the egg. veginer for were the sper are relest wome, were the baby will grow flopen tubs, to Joan the ovar to the wobe.

Catherine

Catherine, her two older sisters and their parents lived in an extremely tidy detached house in a village. I asked Catherine what she liked reading and was told Point horror books and Roald Dahl. She told me that she quite liked science, the best bits being experiments. She didn't like writing up the experiments but liked the cutting out and colouring in of digestion cut-outs.

On both my Year 7 visits, Catherine preferred to be interviewed on her own though she wanted to remain, and did so, for my interview with her mother. Her mother was pleased that Catherine was settling in well and told me that her report was excellent, with an A in science. When I asked how she would describe her daughter, Catherine and her mother looked at each other and smiled. Her mother then said 'She's become much more independent since she went to Pasmoor School. She's grown up in that short space of time. Sometimes it's not what you want. She can be very helpful . . . sometimes she says no which is very typical of the age . . . she occasionally does things we don't like and then she gets grounded'. At this Catherine rejoined 'I haven't for ages' and her mother acknowledged 'No' (to Catherine) and (to me) 'she wouldn't be a child if she didn't occasionally do things wrong'.

Clive

Clive only joined the group in December of Year 7, he and his parents having travelled to England from South Africa. The family was living in a terraced row of bungalows in a village and Clive's room was also the main room in the small house. I noticed that there wasn't a book visible. Clive usually cycled the ten-mile round journey to Pasmoor School unless he had a guitar lesson, when his father took him in the car. Neither of his parents were at home for the first interview. His mother was English and his father German and Clive told me that he spoke these two languages and Afrikaans fluently or near fluently.

I found out that Clive was 13 years old, a full year older than the others in the group. He told me that he was very good at 'mercy'. I didn't know what he meant so he explained that it is the game where you lock fingers and try to bend the other person's fingers back (presumably until they cry 'mercy').

On my second visit, both of Clive's parents were there as well as he. At one point Clive and his mother were out of the room getting me an orange juice and his father spoke about how he was aware that Clive was more physical than other pupils – I understood this to mean in terms of how to settle arguments. He said that this was due to the culture in which he had been brought up. When Clive and his mother returned, Clive's parents told me how they found England so much less aggressive than South Africa.

Edward

Edward, his parents and younger brother lived in a detached village house. His room was decorated with daggers and other weapons, calendars and a number of model aeroplanes. He told me about how to paint these and how they were arranged to show a dogfight. There were about 40 books, almost half of them annuals such as *The Beano* and *The Dandy*.

Edward told me that he had found the science lessons 'Enjoyable. I enjoy science and maths lessons. There's only one part of science I don't like and that's the writing part. I enjoy the experiments'. When I asked his mother her opinions of Pasmoor School she said 'So far, so good. Edward has a sequencing problem, a learning difficulty . . . All schools give us the same old story. We intend to go into Pasmoor School next year . . . Edward does a lot of work on the computer . . . spelling awful and handwriting . . . spelling better when he uses the computer'.

When I asked Edward's mother what her hopes were for him for the future she replied: 'I'd like him to be a confident adult and obviously to be able to get a job at the end of it. He hopes to go into computing which is what his father does. At one point he wanted to be a vet, but obviously that's out of the question. I'd like him to go to university . . . Be happy . . . Biggest worry is GCSEs . . . getting him more time perhaps'. She then asked me about whether one could get more time for GCSEs because of 'sequencing dyslexia' and we talked about this for a bit. 'I know he's one of those kids who will do all right because he's got that sort of personality . . . He has that sort of mastery . . .' She then told me about Edward's ability to sell things – for example, at a school bazaar, and also raffle tickets to someone whom no one else could sell to.

At school, Edward stood out as a most individual character. On 13 February, for example, he spent several minutes trying to get me to sign what was in effect a Pupils' Bill of Rights as we waited for Stephen Benton to arrive and start the lesson. I went through each statement carefully and signed about a quarter of them. Some of them seemed eminently sensible. For instance, he wanted 'brake' (break) patrolled. I asked why. ''Cos there's lots of drugs and smoking and things'. Others were humorous. For example, he wanted long assemblies – not something for which most pupils gather petitions. When I asked him why he replied, admittedly with a certain logic, 'So the lessons would be shorter'.

George

George was one of the first pupils in the group whose name I learnt. It would have been difficult not to. He bubbled with apparently endless energy. It was George who early on cheerfully asked Stephen Benton whether the safety screen carefully positioned for a demonstration was 'a riot shield'. It was George who surprised himself by accidentally snapping his ruler in half. It was George who flicked things at the fluorescent lights. And it was George who was one of the first pupils not to do his homework.

George lived with his parents and two younger sisters in a large farmhouse on a working farm in a village. His favourite subjects were 'Technology 'cos you can do all sorts of things in that, expressive arts, science sometimes'. Further questioning revealed that George liked the practical work in science but not 'the writing . . . too many words'.

George found it difficult to describe himself. His father tried to help by saying to him 'Well, are you intelligent or stupid or . . .?' George answered

'Well, I'm not exactly intelligent, but I have my ways of being clever'. I said I thought that was a marvellous answer. His mother said 'He's always taken an avid interest in everything' and his father continued 'Like me – always wanted to know how things work'. George agreed and then enthusiastically told me how when he was 6 years old he took a radio-controlled car apart, and then found he couldn't put it back together again.

Ian

Ian lived with his parents and two brothers, one younger and one older, in a detached house in central Cambridge. He had been to an independent primary school of national repute before going to Pasmoor School and told me that he couldn't think of any science he had done during Year 7 that he hadn't already done. However, he had found it 'interesting'. Although he had 'done it all before' it had been 'good to recap'. He told me that he liked maths and science but not PE (physical education).

On my first visit Ian told me that he liked 'listening to music, playing on the computer and watching TV'. I asked him what sort of music and he said 'heavy metal' specifically mentioning 'Iron Maiden and Metallica'. He was happy to show me his room and we passed his father, at the computer, on the upstairs landing.

The thing I noticed almost immediately about Ian's room was an impressive-looking telescope pointing out of the window. Ian told me he used it for looking at the stars and the Moon. His room also had some Moon and star maps on the bookshelf. Ian told me that he didn't read much, his favourite books being *Star Trek* ones. There must have been 30–40 books in the room.

On my second visit when I asked both parents what their hopes were for Ian's future, his father began 'I myself see a lot of myself in Ian so it's a rather biased view!' He said this cheerfully and I responded 'You see an outstanding future for Ian!' and both parents laughed genuinely. His father continued 'So I would like to see him do well in science. I feel maths is very important, so I'm pleased he's doing well in maths. So I'd like him to get on well in that. I'd like to see him become less shy'. His mother then added 'And more confident . . . Like all parents, a bit worrying, the uncertainty, the worry of falling between stools in the school system and nobody noticing'.

Jack

Jack lived with his younger brother and parents in a village bungalow. His room was decorated with posters of Iron Maiden, Metallica and various space fantasy games such as 'Frontier Elite II'. Jack told me that he spent a lot of time playing hobby and computer games and these were in evidence in his room as were about 35–50 books. I asked him what he liked reading. His favourites were horror books, specifically R.L. Stine.

Describing himself, Jack said 'I like music a lot. Well, I'm not that musical.

I try to be friendly. I think I laugh a lot. Me and Ian hang around a lot together. I enjoy computer games. So does Ian. We've got a lot in common. And I enjoy drama as well'. His father described Jack as 'Intelligent and thoughtful and . . . considerate'. His mother said 'I think he's quite independent minded . . . He can be a bit of a worrier . . . Rather precocious, walked at 9 months . . . A bit of an introvert'.

Jane

Jane, her parents and her younger brother had come to England from the USA for a year. For this period, her father, a reproductive physiologist, was on sabbatical at a scientific institute attached to Cambridge University. After just over a term, Jane's parents decided to remove her from Pasmoor School and educate her at home for the remainder of the year. Jane told me that her mother taught her each day from 8.40 to 2.40 with a one-hour break at lunchtime.

On my first visit to their home, two months after the start of her home teaching, Jane's father described Pasmoor School as 'awful'. He painted a graphic picture of major discipline problems there with pupils unable to learn anything in lessons as teachers sat with their heads slumped in their hands. Jane's parents felt that she was falling behind her contemporaries back in the States and wasn't learning as much as she should be. They also found unsatisfactory some of the language used by the pupils and, indeed, even some of the teachers. Jane's father told me of one teacher who used the word 'bloody' as a swear word when referring to Jesus.

Jane's parents both had a deep Christian faith and Jane had gone to a Christian school in the States before coming to England. When I asked them what their hopes were for Jane her father said 'Our main hope is she ends up having all the training and ability so she can do what she wants to do'. He went on to talk briefly about Jane wanting to be either a doctor or a marine biologist. Jane's mother then said that she wanted that Jane 'always puts the Lord first in her life and does want He wants her to do'. Her father agreed and added 'If she always puts the Lord first, she'll be able to do what I said'.

Her father described Jane as being 'very capable . . . Has the ability to do anything she sets her mind to do, very loving and has a sweet disposition'. Her mother then added 'She's always been strong willed. Has always had her own opinion and voiced it. She's always been a leader among the little kids'.

Jane said that her favourite subject was science and that she had begun to write a book on 'The Human Body'. On my second visit, after she had been educated at home for six months, I asked her how she was finding the science at home. 'I'm really, really enjoying it. I've learnt a lot in science . . . I like doing experiments . . . but I do need the textbooks. At Pasmoor School we did too many experiments'. Jane explained to me that at home she would do about one experiment a week. I asked her for an example of an experiment she had done at home and she told me about making volcanoes. They had made a volcano out of mud, soda, vinegar and orange colouring and had used a finger to make the hole.

On my first visit Jane's mother had shown me an American school science textbook that they were using to teach Jane. I noticed a sentence in the textbook referring to amber being millions of years old and asked Jane's parents how they felt about that. Jane's mother said they had told Jane that wasn't correct but had carried on using the textbook.

Liz

Liz, her younger sister and her parents were over in England from the USA for nine months while her father, who worked on AIDS and development research, was on a sabbatical at a scientific institute attached to Cambridge University. On my first and only visit Liz came across as self-confident and articulate. She liked Cambridge, where they were living, and felt it was much safer than where she lived in the States where she didn't like walking around because of all the guns and gangs.

Liz told me that 'I like going over to friends' houses, going into town, see whatever we want and buy whatever we want. I like discos'. I asked about these. She went to the graduate discos at one of the Cambridge colleges. She told me that she played a lot on the computer and was friends with Mary.

Liz was also a ready source of information about others in the science class I was watching. She showed me a ring she was wearing which had been given to her by one of the boys and told me all about another of the boys trying to kiss one of the girls several times when they were going out. 'Plus he likes boys, and boys pretty much hate him because he tried to kiss one of them . . . So many things going on that the teachers don't even notice'.

Liz's father was happy for me to post them the questions for the second visit. This I did and, after a follow-up letter from me, Liz sent me a handwritten letter which included the following, verbatim, extracts:

> The science program at [my present school] is quite boring from the one at Pasmoor School because there a rarly any hands on experiments its quite boring compare with to Pasmoor School. [Pasmoor School] has the most exciting science department in the world. The good the things about Pasmoor School were the experiments. But because [my present school] doesn't do many experiments Pasmoor School better in that department. But one thing [my present school] does do is their in the USA globe program so in a couple of week we'll go out every day and look whats going on outside. The bad things about [my present school] are the lack of Science equipment so thay cannot conduct very good experiments. I've changed quite a bit since I was in England I not so uptight about things and I have much more self-confidence. At [my present school] science sucks. In the summer Mary from England is going to come over and visit am going to go to camp, and hang out with my friends, and party.

Marc

Marc lived with his mother, stepfather and elder sister in a semi-detached house in a village. Marc was a keen footballer and also played a number of musical instruments. His room had a number of football trophies of his, about which he was rather modest. His mother described him as 'fun loving. He can be caring. He can be very untidy . . . He's active. He doesn't like to sit still for long. [Pause.] Sometimes I think he's shy . . . and lacking in confidence'. His mother also talked about Marc being 'the man of the family until [Marc's step-father] arrived'.

When I asked Marc about his reading he talked about comic and football annuals and ghost and adventure books. He thought that scientists spent their time 'sharing their experiments that they do and their results and helping people understand like how to do the experiments'.

Martin

Martin lived with his parents in a terraced village house. His first love was sports. He played a lot of cricket and football and his room had a number of football posters as well as one of a tiger and one showing rare breeds of farm animals.

When I asked his father how he thought Martin was getting on in science he replied 'To be perfectly honest, I don't know . . . and I don't believe in getting involved in kids' homework. And I've told him if he can't do something he's got to see you or whoever . . . If it's something to do with school I'd rather he asked the teachers'. I asked his father what Martin had been like when he was younger and he told me of an incident when the head teacher of Martin's junior school had summoned him from the golf-course saying that Martin had gone 'berserk'. Martin's father said that it was all 'a lot of fuss over nothing'. Apparently there had been some incident during which a smaller child had got hurt.

There were a number of occasions when Martin tried to cause trouble in the Year 7 lessons. For instance, in the first term he told me that 'Mr Benton called you Mr Pooee' to which I replied 'I doubt it'. Later in the same lesson Michael broke a beaker and Martin announced to Stephen 'He just broke it, deliberately'. In the second term he was patronizing to Peter when Peter had told me that his family were going on a holiday to Butlins, which caused Peter to be aggrieved. In the third term there was an occasion when Michael fell heavily and Martin's reaction was to burst out laughing.

Mary

Mary lived with her mother, stepfather and younger brother and sister in an extended cottage in a village. In class I had noticed that she sometimes managed to read non-science books for quite long periods – *Babysitter's Nightmare*, for example. When I asked her at the first interview about her reading she mentioned R.L. Stine, *Dracula* and another horror author. I asked her what she liked about horror books and she said the fact that they made her nervous. She also liked the *Sweet Valley High* series of school books and told me about the breaking of the Stone Table in *The Lion, The Witch and The Wardrobe*. In addition to reading, Mary volunteered that she liked 'Guides, swimming, dancing, art, playing the violin'.

I asked what she did at weekends and she said that she spent most of Sundays doing homework – her mother explained that this was because Mary's life was so full during the week. I said that that sounded very efficient and Mary's mother described her daughter as being organized. Mary also mentioned staying with friends at weekends or going into Cambridge, for example to buy clothes. She then launched into needing new jeans and another top and some shoes this Saturday which her stepfather gently and partially deflected.

Mary's stepfather talked about the fact that they had thought quite carefully a full year in advance about which secondary school Mary should go to. They had investigated two other state schools – 'they sell drugs outside the school gate there' Mary commented dismissively of one of them – and the private sector. Mary told me she wasn't keen on the idea of private schools and described one local private educational establishment of national renown as a 'stuck up school'.

Because I hadn't heard her say a great deal in lessons I hadn't appreciated how quick-witted Mary was until I met her. On my first visit she talked amusingly about the way the school bus was driven and on my second, in response to my asking her how she had found the science lessons so far, she produced a succinct and pretty devastating critique of Stephen Benton's teaching style.

Michael

Michael lived with his two younger brothers and his mother in a detached village cottage. It was 18 February on the day of my first interview and Michael cheerfully showed me numerous paintings of his and a valentine's card he had given his mother. When I asked him what he liked doing out of school he promptly replied 'Reading. I spend most of my time reading'. He told me about books on animals, fiction and history and talked about the *Narnia* books, Rosemary Sutcliffe, Ronald Welch and Willard Price.

On my first visit we somehow got onto the possibility of the four of them moving to New Zealand to be with Michael's mother's boyfriend. In his mother's presence Michael described this as 'Horrid . . . It's awful'. His mother told me that she was just recently divorced. On my second visit there was a 'For Sale' notice outside the house. When I got to the last question ('What are your hopes for next year?') I said to Michael that I asked this question of everyone I interviewed, though I realized it might be a particularly significant question for him. His mother laughed at the question and Michael answered

'I hope we can go to New Zealand and build a new life there because our life has deteriorated since Mum and Dad got divorced'. I said 'It sounds as if you're trying to be very positive'.

Michael told me a bit about his getting 'bullied' at school and added '. . . sometimes I've finished all the worksheets when some people are still on the first one . . . I get teased in most subjects'. His mother said 'Despite the bullying he's relaxed a lot'. She went on to talk about Michael being 'terribly bright . . . arty, dreamy child . . . he is academic'. Michael proudly told me about his getting some art prize at Pasmoor School and his mother told me about his getting a bronze certificate at the maths olympiad. I told them I was impressed as I had been entered for this at school and had got through the first two rounds but had never got as far as getting a medal.

In science lessons, Michael, who often worked on his own, displayed a rare ability. He came top in the 'Energy' test, discovered for himself the principle of dark field microscope illumination, succeeded in extracting the word 'mitochondria' from me by insisting I tell him what the unlabelled dots in the published drawing of a cheek cell were, told me with enthusiasm about a sheep dissection he had witnessed and showed awe at such things as the energy transfers involved in a lamp lighting. Once he told me with delight about the way in which the expansion of something with heat allowed a thermometer to be invented and on another occasion he explained to me some of the consequences for animal welfare of the new breed of sheep, Texels, which, he told me, have twice the muscle mass in their legs of conventional breeds.

Nicky

Nicky lived with her parents, younger sister and younger brother in a semi-detached house in a village. Ten days before my first visit she asked me if I liked Hobnuts. I said I did and a plate of tasty biscuits duly appeared when I arrived for the interview. Indeed, during the lesson after this visit she slipped me a foil-wrapped package of chocolate chip biscuits. (There are certain benefits from carrying out educational research.)

Nicky was as easy to talk with in her home as she was vivacious in school. On my first visit I soon found out, as we played with a hamster, that she had acted in *Charlie and the Chocolate Factory* and had taken the lead role in *Joseph and His Amazing Technicolour Dream Coat*. In addition, she played the flute, did aerobics, went to Guides, did ballet and was a serious gymnast. She had three sessions a week of gymnastics, each of three hours. At one point she had joined the national squad and trained five days a week but she had found this rather boring – they had to do the same thing again and again and again – and then she got an injury, so she had gone back to three times a week. One of her parents said 'So now you'll never be world champion' and Nicky agreed with this quite cheerfully.

On my second visit Nicky said of herself 'I'm helpful. I can listen to people. And people can approach me quite easily. I don't tell anyone if you tell me a secret. I'm trustworthy – not perfect, but you know'. I reflected this back to her and she added 'I can be funny, you know, not always sad and I like to have a laugh with my friends and go out with them and everything. That's it really'.

On both visits Nicky said that within science she liked biology the most. She saw scientists as 'trying to find out information to get the answer . . . and trying to find different sorts of medicine and cure disease . . . and information to help people'.

Paul

Paul's parents were the only parents in the study who knew anything about me before the study started. They worship regularly in a Baptist congregation in a village where I had done services at the parish (i.e. Church of England) Church. I had met them previously on at least one occasion when there had been a joint service between the two congregations. Paul's mother reminded me of this when I phoned up to make the initial appointment.

Indeed, Christianity played an important and pervasive role in much of Paul's family life. At the first interview I arrived to find the family at dinner and two children of a minister eating with them. As I interviewed Paul after the meal, much of the separate conversation between his father and these two children was about a Christian youth group in which they were heavily involved. At the second interview, in answer to my question 'What are your hopes for Paul for the future?', Paul's mother replied 'I want him to do what-ever he's happy at doing. I just feel the Lord's got their lives planned . . . It would be nice if they went to university . . . but I'd just like them to be happy at what they're doing . . . All we really want is for the kids to be happy going to Church'. I conducted the second interview in the second half of August and Paul told me that he had 'been camping out last week at a Christian camp'. 'How did that go?' I asked.'Quite well. Quite a lot were Christians and quite a few became Christians'.

Paul was a quiet boy in class and he wasn't very chatty with me in the two Year 7 interviews. He became more communicative, though, when we got onto hobbies. In addition to playing hockey and football, he told me that he made planes. He also enjoyed fishing and read fishing magazines.

Paul thought that scientists spent their time 'Trying to make new medicines and cures and making food very quickly . . . testing on animals things . . .' In his science lessons Paul enjoyed the experiments but found 'a lot of writing . . . boring'.

Peter

Peter's mother didn't want me to come and interview Peter during Year 7 so it wasn't until Year 8 that I found out that Peter lived with his mother, step-father and elder brother in a detached village home.

In school Peter came across as extrovert. He would chat with me before the start of lessons about playing football and told me about his birthday presents and going to visit his father. He would chat with just about anyone in lessons too. And joke, and pretend to be asleep, and sing, and take his ball-point to pieces, etc. He and Marc were also the first two pupils I saw being given a detention, which they got for making silly noises, while Peter was the first pupil I saw sent out of class – for talking during a video.

Rebecca

Rebecca lived with her parents and her younger brother and sister in a semi detached village house. Her favourite subject was art and she liked writing 'poems and stories and stuff'. As we played with her current hamster – the first one having lived almost till the age of three – she told me that she liked cats and swimming. Indeed, the family cat had come and sat on me soon after I arrived. I mentioned books and she offered to take me up to her room. There must have been over 100 books including fiction and non-fiction. Her current reading, by her bed, was a hardback book about badgers and other animals.

Rebecca offered to show me her drawings and we spent quite a while looking at them including a fine one of a church and three lovely ones of cats. We spent some 20 minutes in her room and only went downstairs again at my instigation. She told me that she enjoyed all aspects of science, specifically mentioning animals, plants, chemistry and space. She talked with real enthusiasm about the first 'Rainbow fizz' lesson and then talked about the notion that the universe goes on for ever: 'Sort of an overpowering feeling; the world being so small compared to this massive universe. [Pause:] And then what's going to happen? . . . Earth evolving and apes evolving into men or whether God did it. I respect people's beliefs but if people have got evidence for a Big Bang . . .'

On my second visit, Rebecca, with genuine insouciance, was stymied when I asked her to describe herself: 'I don't know. Umm. [Pause.] I haven't a clue. I don't know'. Eventually she said 'I love animals and I don't really like to see them mistreated' and launched into a long story about a friend of hers who had 'rescued' a horse following an unsuccessful prosecution against the horse's owners after the horse had been left for long periods without food or water. When I asked her parents the same question, in Rebecca's presence, her father said 'Very strong-willed . . . a kind nature . . . very honest'. Her mother said that she was 'a bit of a dreamer . . . very mature' and her father added 'independent, outgoing. When you were younger, people were absolutely amazed at how you were able to converse with an adult'.

I asked Rebecca's parents how they thought she was getting on at school and her mother said that she had told one of the teachers that she thought of her daughter as 'not very academic'. The teacher, who disagreed with this assessment 'almost threw me out of the school', she added somewhat ruefully. Certainly, Rebecca was doing well at science. For instance, on the end-of-unit test on 'Bodies', she was one of only two pupils to get 20 out of 20 (the other being Burt).

Richard

Richard lived with his parents and younger brother in a detached village home which his parents had designed themselves. His brother had moderate to severe learning difficulties and attended a special school. Richard said his favourite subject was technology (metal and woodwork) especially when they used the equipment. Wednesday was the day he liked most but Monday was boring because they had to copy from books and write. His second favourite subject was science while music was good because they actually did things.

I mentioned his room and Richard was keen to show it to me. There were photographs of *Discovery* (i.e. the space shuttle) on the wall and it turned out he had been to Florida four times and had seen *Discovery* taking off once. There were about 40–70 books but Richard told me that he didn't read much. I commented on a Meccano model he had made and he enthusiastically showed me a Technics model of a truck he had made with an air-controlled pump. He also showed me some volcanic rock he had got when visiting Lanzarote. I said (truthfully) that I didn't know where Lanzarote was and we tried unsuccessfully to find it on the world map above the head of his bed.

Richard was very conscientious in his attitude towards school work. When I asked him how he had found his first year at Pasmoor School he said 'It has been quite hard . . . Teachers . . . have been quite helpful'. He went on, without my asking him about it, to tell me that he hoped to do well in Year 8. His hopes for next year were to 'Do better. Umm. Enjoy it. Do the homework successfully. Get good marks. Good things really'. His mother described him as 'Basically quiet, shy, considerate' and later added 'mischievous'. His father said that 'He suffers from lacking confidence; he struggles'.

From the first day that I observed the group's science lessons, Richard was teased or bullied by others. A pun was made on his surname – rather as if someone whose surname was 'Desmond' was endlessly called 'Dusty'. Two of the boys, in particular, often hit him. They also kicked him, blamed him when equipment wouldn't work, refused to share instructions with him, were rude to him about his clothes and insulted him in other ways. As far as I could see, Richard did his best to respond to all this cheerfully and with occasional, somewhat half-hearted, self-defence.

Robert

Robert lived with his elder sister and parents in a detached house on the outskirts of a village. The family had moved there because they wanted a large garden for their greyhounds. Greyhounds played an important part in their lives. In addition to the two at the bottom of the garden which they kept for racing, they had two retired greyhounds in beautiful condition which padded majestically round the house on my two Year 7 visits.

Robert, who was always very quiet in science lessons, was quiet at home too and I didn't at first succeed in getting him to say a great deal during the interviews. When I asked his parents what Robert had been like when he was younger his mother said 'The thing I remember the most when he was very young . . . he never spoke at playgroup the whole year, not even to the supervisor. I remember being worried about him going to primary school'. She then told me a tale about a child who came, with his mother, to their house during the year that Robert was in playgroup. On hearing Robert speak the child exclaimed 'Mummy, Robert can talk!' Robert's mother then added that Robert was now 'not as shy as I thought he might be'.

It turned out that this was the second academic research project in which Robert had been a participant. His mother told me that because of his shyness he had been chosen for a project at Madingley (University of Cambridge Sub-Department of Animal Behaviour). I told her this was where I had done my PhD. The research had involved lots of questionnaires and then she had had to take Robert to Madingley and leave him in a room while they videoed him. Robert couldn't remember any of this. I asked if they had ever told her what the point of the research was but they hadn't.

Robert said he was keen on fishing. He told me about some of the fish he had caught, including a 2lb chub. He brought down from his bedroom three books on fishing, all of which were detailed and written for adults. Robert also told me he was keen on playing with the computer. I asked whether he used it for computer games. He said yes but that he also used it for word-processing. It turned out that he was writing a book on fishing.

Rodney

Rodney, his elder brother, older sister and his parents lived in a large house near to the centre of Cambridge. On my first visit Rodney's mother brought up the issue of his dyslexia before I had begun my questions, telling me that Rodney had spent the year before coming to Pasmoor School at a boarding school that catered especially for pupils with dyslexia. In answer to my question about how he was finding Pasmoor School compared to his previous school, Rodney told me that at Pasmoor School he liked working with George because 'he has a reading and writing problem'.

In addition to skiing, going out on his bike, sailing and playing squash, Rodney told me that he liked making things. He had made a number of bird tables from scrap. His mother told me that he had made £100 from selling them. More recently he had been making some wind chimes out of copper, his father having shown him how. Rodney had also built various things including a cabin.

On my second visit, in answer to my question about how they would describe Rodney, his mother replied 'Oh, oh gosh. He's creative. He's got a brilliant personality. Incredibly naughty. He's got a perception of people beyond his years . . .' His father described him as 'Gregarious, outgoing and willing . . . Determined'. Rodney's dyslexia featured strongly when I asked his parents what their hopes were for him. His father said 'Depends how far he gets really with all the reading. Writing not so important really . . . because of technological advances'. His mother noted 'At the moment . . . we always talk as though Rodney will leave school at the age of 16 . . . But Rodney is a survivor. So we have no worries. I used to despair when he was first diagnosed'.

Rodney's mother went on to tell me about how, recently, Rodney had gone round five shops trying to persuade them to give him a job but they hadn't because he was too small. His father then told me about how Rodney and a friend had succeeded in collecting £3 by searching the grates outside Trinity College. They had even managed to get given 20p by someone who thought they had lost their own money.

Sue

Sue told me that her mother was too busy preparing to have another baby for me to go to their home and do the Year 7 interviews. So it wasn't until Year 8 that I got to visit Sue, her several brothers and sisters and her parents in a small semi-detached village house.

In class the main things I noticed about Sue were that she seemed to have a quiet personality and was away considerably more often than other pupils.

Comment on pupil differences

When the pupils had flooded into their science laboratory for their first science lesson I had had a sudden irrational feeling that there weren't any important differences between them (see p. 1). By the end of Year 7 it seemed remarkable to me that I could have felt like that. The pupils had become 21 individuals to me.

I could write, for example, about their varied reading interests. While, in common with larger surveys of children's reading at this time, their reading showed a general move away from the classics that were read in the early 1970s (when the five mostly widely read books by 12- to 13-year-olds were reported as being, in descending order, *Little Women*, *Black Beauty*, *Treasure Island*, *The Lion, the Witch and the Wardrobe* and *Jane Eyre*) to a broader diet based more on Point Horror authors such as R.L. Stine (Benton 1995), there were interesting individual differences only partly related to gender.

However, because my particular interest in this study is science education, I was especially interested in individual differences that caused me to wonder whether some, more than others, would enjoy and do well at science. Would Ian's telescope be indicative of a genuine interest in science? Would Rebecca keep her open-minded wondering about the universe?

I was also struck by the fact that at least three of the pupils (Burt, Edward and Rodney) had dyslexia. In each case there was parental concern about the consequences this might have for their education and future prospects.

Finally, I was sorry that three of the pupils would not be returning for Year

8. Jane had only lasted a term at school before being withdrawn by her parents to be educated at home. I would have loved to have known how Jane's education subsequently developed. It was Jane, alone of all the pupils, who felt that science lessons could have too many experiments. I found myself wondering whether this was said in loyalty (conscious or otherwise) to her parents. Home schooling can provide a volcano made out of mud, soda, vinegar and orange colouring, but it's difficult for it to provide the full range of scientific equipment and materials available in a secondary school science laboratory, even if one's father is an academic scientist.

Liz, too, was heading back to the USA as her father, like Jane's, returned from a sabbatical at Cambridge. In fact, largely on account of her friendship with Mary, I kept in touch with Liz for some time after she had returned to the States. She had major (successful) back surgery and her parents split up. Of particular interest to me was the way she contrasted the abundance of practical work at Pasmoor School with her American experiences. In July 1997 (i.e. at the end of what would have been Year 9) she told me how, in contrast to her English experience, 'we're finally getting into labs . . . Really funny because she [i.e. the teacher] was like saying "This is a beaker" . . .'

Finally, Michael was setting off with his mother and younger brothers to a new life in New Zealand. It was Jenny, to whom I am married, who asked me why I had chosen 'Michael', my name, as his pseudonym. I admitted to her that I hadn't thought about it. On reflection, I wonder whether subconsciously I saw some similarities between Michael and myself, as least as far as his academic gifts, his delight at knowledge and his occasional social isolation were concerned.

Key points

- During Year 7 pupils were introduced by their teacher to the content of science, the process of science and the language of science.
- At the beginning of Year 7 girls and boys were equally likely to engage in scientific talk with their teacher. As the year went on, girls participated significantly less in such talk.
- As revealed by my interview with him, girls made less of an impression on their Year 7 teacher than did boys.
- At the beginning of Year 7 there was a strict, self-imposed segregation between girls and boys. As the year wore on, though, interactions between some of the girls and some of the boys increased greatly in frequency, type and purpose.
- Interviews with the pupils and their parents revealed considerable variety in such things as: what the pupils read, their hobbies, what their parents thought of them, how they felt about science lessons and the importance of religion in their home.

3

Year 8: 'George was eager . . . but putting pen to paper – forget it'

> . . . because knowledge has to be assimilated, and that takes time.
> (Aristotle [n.d.]1976: 233)

'Setting': different ability classes

On their return to Pasmoor School at the beginning of Year 8, after the summer holidays, the pupils I was particularly interested in – most of whom were noticeably larger after six weeks of growth – were placed, along with other pupils, into four different science sets. Stephen Benton was in charge of a Foundation class (lowest ability), Helen Coombs was in charge of a Merit class (middle ability) and Hannah Thomson and James Western were each in charge of a Special class (top ability). In addition, Year 8 also had five other science classes, made up of one Foundation, two Merit and two Special classes. However, none of these five classes contained any of the pupils I had been following in Year 7.

Most schools, at some point, wrestle with the issue of setting. The principal arguments in favour of setting stress that with sets teachers can target their teaching more precisely while pupils perhaps work best alongside their intellectual equals. In addition, it is felt by many teachers that, whatever the arguments in favour of mixed-ability teaching, such teaching becomes more and more difficult as pupils age.

Perhaps the fundamental argument against setting is that it disadvantages those placed in lower and even middle sets. Certainly, it is far more common for parents to want their children to be raised a set rather than lowered one. Yet if parents accepted the argument that setting was in the interests of each child, whatever her or his abilities, this should not be the case. Classic educational research has documented what is known as the 'Pygmalion effect'. That is, setting becomes a self-fulfilling prophecy. Teachers tend to treat pupils differently simply by virtue of the sets they are in – pupils in top sets have more expected of them than pupils in bottom sets.

This is the case even if pupils are deliberately placed in the 'wrong' sets. As a result, for example, so called 'low-ability' pupils placed in top sets do far better than they would have done in bottom sets. Indeed, in the first term of my study, back in Year 7, Stephen Benton told me, without my asking him about setting, that he had often noticed that when the pupils were set for other subjects, especially mathematics, the pupils put in the lower sets then got discouraged in their science lessons, even though science was still being taught in mixed-ability groups.

Another argument against setting is that the evidence on which children are initially allocated to sets is often weak. In the worst instances, pupils are put in low sets simply because of their poor behaviour. Even without this being the case, any attempt to measure differences between pupils as soon as they have been set (i.e. before the Pygmalion effect has come into play) is likely to reveal a very considerable overlap between sets. In principle this should not matter too much, provided pupils are frequently moved up or down sets. However, this rarely happens. Teachers are wary of breaking up social relationships and, typically, only a small number of pupil movements between sets are made, often only at the end of a school year. In fact, moves between sets were more frequent at Pasmoor School than is often the case, and pupils were never put in lower sets for behavioural reasons.

These disadvantages of setting may have a particular impact on boys, in part simply because boys are generally overrepresented in low-ability sets. This is the case nationally and was true at Pasmoor School too. Year 8 is a time when some pupils have problems with motivation and engagement (Rudduck *et al.* 1998) and some researchers have argued that the seeds of the disaffection which certain males end up having towards schooling in particular and authority in general are fuelled by boys' experiences in Year 8 (Bleach *et al.* 1996).

Halfway through the year, in February, the pupils sat their Year 8 science examination. The results for the four sets I was interested in are shown in Figure 3.1. The maximum possible mark was 66. Pupils were told that there was the following correspondence between marks and National Curriculum levels:

- a mark of 53 or over equated to a National Curriculum Level 6;
- a mark of between 38 and 52 equated to a Level 5;
- a mark of between 28 and 37 equated to a Level 4;
- a mark of 27 or less equated to a Level 3.

In England and Wales, National Curriculum levels have been used in national assessments since 1989. These assessments are universally known as 'SATs' (Standard Assessment Tests/Tasks) and are administered at the ends of Year 2 (i.e. to 7-year-olds), Year 6 (11-year-olds) and Year 9 (14-year-olds). Each level is defined by criteria that are specific to each subject. It is expected that the 'normal' (whatever that means) performance should be a Level 1 on entry to school at age 5 (i.e. at the end of Year 0, as it were). Every two years thereafter, normal performance should increase by one level. This would

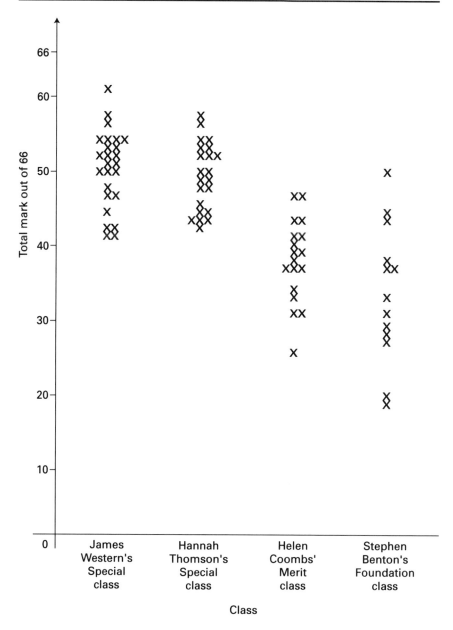

Figure 3.1 The performance of the four Year 8 classes I was observing in the Year 8 science examination in February

mean Level 2 at the end of Year 2 (the Key Stage 1 SATs), Level 4 at the end of Year 6 (the Key Stage 2 SATs) and Level 5 or 6 at the end of Year 9 (the Key Stage 3 SATs). In February of Year 8 one would therefore expect most pupils to be performing at Level 5. This would equate to scoring in the low- to mid-40s on the Pasmoor School Year 8 science test.

It is noticeable that:

- Pupils in the two Special sets scored equally impressively. The mean marks for the two Special sets were 49.5 (75 per cent) and 50.4 (76 per cent).
- There was a very considerable overlap between the marks of the pupils in the Merit and Foundation groups. The mean mark for the Merit set was 38.9 (59 per cent); the mean mark for the Foundation set was 34.3 (52 per cent).
- However defined (standard deviation, range, inter-quartile range), the Foundation set showed the greatest range of marks.

Stephen Benton's Foundation class

Stephen Benton's Foundation class contained just 13 pupils, 4 of them girls and 9 of them boys. Four of the pupils (all boys – Clive, George, Peter and Rodney) had been in the class I had watched in Year 7. However, Clive left the school halfway through the year. I received conflicting acounts as to where he and his family had gone and attempts by me to contact them were unsuccessful.

Stephen Benton had been at Pasmoor School for 17 years. Outside of school his interests included gardening, wine-making, socializing and reading. When I asked him what he was 'trying to achieve in science lessons', he replied:

> I think the objectives are whatever the actual curriculum is . . . I think also basic skills in science; doing practicals or writing or whatever it is; organizational skills . . . sense of interest and excitement though that's distorted by the syllabus, of course. I think those are the main ones. And I suppose some of the teamwork elements as they work in groups – social skills.

Some of the implications of setting were brought home to me in the very first double lesson of the Foundation class that I saw soon after the beginning of Year 8. The class was working in small groups on the topic of pollution and when I arrived to find the pupils lining up outside Stephen Benton's lab, Peter enthusiastically spent a good minute telling me about the apparatus they had put out last time at different places round the school to measure the amount of dust there was.

Five minutes into the lesson there was an announcement over the school loudspeaker system in which the teacher who was talking used the word 'clockwise'. Peter asked out loud 'What does "clockwise" mean?' and Stephen told him.

Much of the lesson was spent making posters on which each group of pupils was to record what the pupils in the group had done and what they had found out. The whole feel of the lesson, particularly in its pace and the intellectual demands made on the pupils, seemed noticeably different from the other classes I was seeing in Year 8. At one point, one of the boys spent much of ten minutes using a hole punch to punch a large number of holes.

By 10.15 a.m., after the pupils had spent 65 minutes on their posters, the only writing on the one done jointly by George, Rodney and one other boy was:

CO^2 traps ultra violet light
These are Our results

The other notable feature about this lesson was that it was the first one where I saw a learning support assistant in action in the normal classroom. There had been some occasions in Year 7 when George, Paul, Peter and Rodney (all boys) had been withdrawn from the classroom and provided with help. In Year 8, help was provided more frequently and regularly and in the normal classroom.

Lakisha Mistry had been a learning support assistant at Pasmoor School for seven years and had previously worked there as a youth leader for ten years. When I asked her what she was trying to achieve in science lessons she replied:

Umm. Well, I think in a way I am a reinforcer of what's being taught by the teacher. Sometimes I'm just trying to get over to them what they're being taught so that they'll be interested . . . My job varies from class to class depending on the teacher. I sometimes feel I'm having to be too much of a discipline figure in that class . . . not in our job description . . . which, if I remember rightly, we wrote ourselves! . . . We're not in competition with the members of staff. They're over us . . . we're supposed to work as a team . . . happens most of the time and benefits the class too . . . lots of explaining and modifying the work.

Lakisha was positive about how Pasmoor School made use of its learning support assistants, saying that this was done:

Very well. Much better than they did seven years ago when I started . . . seven years ago . . . just there as if one was in primary school to clear the paint pots up and keep in the background . . . over the years we've shown we're not just there to take the child away with a nosebleed . . . I think our job's better than teaching . . . I think we've become much more accepted as professionals in recent years . . . we adapt work and do special cards and special booklets.

Certainly it was clear in the classroom that learning support assistants at Pasmoor School were greatly appreciated by pupils. Sometimes they would work solely with pupils who had formal statements of special needs (such statements provide a school with additional funding). Sometimes they would help a greater range of children as needs arose. So far as I am aware, the only one of the pupils I was following who had a formal statement of special needs was Rodney. At the end of the year, when I interviewed her, Lakisha spoke warmly of George, Peter and Rodney:

> I think they're all great attention seekers! . . . George: He's a super lad; 13 going on 35. Very worldly-wise but incredibly immature about his work attitude . . . he constantly needs to be kept on task . . . I've found I have to give him time limits . . . and then go back and see how he's getting on . . . Peter: I think he's lovely! He's shown some improvement this year . . . and, again, I find him very bright actually . . . if he finds something he's really interested in . . . Rodney: . . . was a horrible boy in Year 7 and came with a reputation – surprising considering his home background. He was a real handful in Year 7 . . . Year 7 Activities Week showed a completely different side – someone was ill on the coach. He showed a very concerned, caring side. We've had a really good relationship this year.

It was difficult for me to be sure how the pupils in Stephen's class felt about being in what could be termed the 'bottom set'. Without my raising the issue with them, George once said to me, with mild sarcasm but delivered deadpan 'Yeah; we're the intelligent group' to which Rodney responded 'No we're not. We're the thick group'. However, in February (i.e. halfway through the year) after George had complained to a student teacher that some work was too difficult 'because we're the bottom set', I heard Clive asking another boy in the group whether they were indeed in the bottom set. This was also the lesson where Clive volunteered, in all seriousness, the information that if you frightened a Pekinese its eyes pop out, whereupon George, again in all seriousness – so far as I could tell – asked 'If you lengthen your retina and pull out your eye, would it still work?', at which point Lakisha and I raised our eyebrows at each other.

It was also this class, of the four that I was observing, that had the first student teacher teaching them. I arrived at the lesson on 23 January to find the pupils being let into the lab by Lucie Moore for her first lesson on her teaching practice (or 'professional placement' as it is now called). The lesson, in fact, went extremely well but the arrival of a student teacher generally provides an opportunity for certain pupils to treat the lesson as a game in which everything possible is done to deflect the beginning teacher from the intended aim of the lesson.

The lesson was about light and, on asking the pupils about the uses of lasers, the first response was 'For killing little children' and the death theme permeated subsequent answers. At the end of the lesson Lucie gave as their homework 'Find out what is a periscope and where do you use them?' Rodney immediately asked me what a periscope was. I laughed and suggested he ask the teacher if she was happy with him asking me. Rodney didn't but shot off, with Clive, to ask Stephen Benton the same question, only for the two of them to be called back by Lucie before they reached him.

This was also the lesson in which one of the girls in this class burnt her finger on one of the light-bulbs. She wandered over to me, said that it hurt and, on my looking sympathetic, though not saying anything, placed the said finger against my hand. I am reminded of one female student, when I taught at a sixth-form college for 16–18-year-olds, who used occasionally to blow me kisses. It is in such actions that pupils, male and female, explore and push the boundaries of what is acceptable sexual or proto-sexual behaviour. In the case of the sixth-form student, whose behaviour I ignored, she had an affair with one of the other teachers soon after leaving the college.

When I interviewed her at the end of Year 8, Lucie remembered the pupils well:

> George was eager . . . but putting pen to paper – forget it. He would even miss out on a practical to avoid writing. You could reason with Rodney more but they distracted each other, no matter how far apart one moved them . . . Then Peter could be hard-working one day; the next day quite obstreperous . . . But he gets no help with homework. For example . . . periscope: I said 'Look it up in a dictionary' and he said there wasn't one at home.

Lucie also told me about one of the boys who 'was very worried about other people thinking he was gay'. She told me that he had been bullied because of this. The boy in question had gone to see her about this and she had spoken on his behalf to his head of year. However, in the end it had been this boy who had been excluded from school 'because other boys were saying he was gay and he lashed out . . . other boys wouldn't drink from the same drink as him. I confronted the other pupils about this . . .'

Helen Coombs' Merit class

Helen Coombs' Merit class contained 19 pupils, 8 of them girls and 11 of them boys. (As will be clear, this particular year group at Pasmoor School contained a surprising preponderance of boys.) Five of the pupils (Martin, Mary, Paul, Richard and Sue) had been in the class I had watched in Year 7.

Helen Coombs had been at Pasmoor School on and off for 14 years. In fact, she took early retirement at the end of Year 8. Her interests included music, particularly choral work, and she was hoping to be able to spend more time on this now that she was retiring.

In science lessons, Helen told me that:

> I want them to get a genuine interest in what's going on around them . . . for that they have to have some basic knowledge . . . not just in labs, so that when they're outside they can see what's going on. I don't think we've been doing enough [i.e. in science lessons] of everyday things . . .

kitchen . . . factory things . . . we don't do any visits to factories . . . less than we used to do . . . too syllabus-oriented . . . try to find activities that'll create interest . . . because they all get turned on by different things which is why they need different teachers.

In the classroom, Helen seemed to me to combine firmness with friendliness. In the first lesson I saw her teach, on 13 September, she let the pupils in, telling them that she might move some of them if they didn't work hard enough. Later in the lesson she ticked off Martin for wasting her time, threatened the whole class with a test because some pupils were talking, asked a question of one boy knowing that he hadn't been paying attention, and moved one boy. In the same lesson, though, she allowed one of the more self-confident boys to tease her as she teased him about the quality of the excuse he had offered for not having done his homework, and, on walking past the tallest girl in the class, said cheerfully 'You're not allowed to be nearly as tall as me. That's cheating! You've got heels on'.

Nor was Helen reluctant to express her own views about matters scientific and non-scientific. When one rather distinctive boy (who had been statemented for behavioural reasons and at one point during the year seriously hurt another boy by attempting to strangle him) told her during a class where pupils were working individually that he got £6 a week pocket money, she attracted half the class's attention by shrieking 'That's more than I get!'

In a lesson in which she demonstrated the effects of the tar in cigarette smoke on our lungs by drawing air from a lighted cigarette through cotton wool, Helen introduced the apparatus by saying 'So, if you're one of those people who's incredibly stupid enough to smoke you'll be able to see what the smoke is like in your lungs' No rubbish here about pupil autonomy! At the completion of the demonstration, Helen maintained 'I'm not going to lecture you on smoking . . . I want to give you the facts . . . you know which way I want you to make up your minds . . . I don't just want it labelled "cotton wool", I want it labelled "dirty, smelly, horrible old cotton wool"'.

I spent quite a bit of time during Year 8 noting, as I had in Year 7 (see p. 24), which pupils had scientifically meaningful exchanges with their teachers. Aside from the existence or otherwise of generalized gender differences, this exercise brought home to me the extent to which certain individual pupils, both female and male, almost never asked a scientific question or volunteered any scientific information unless asked. In Helen Coombs' class, Paul was especially reticent.

There is, though, a fundamental problem with such quantitative research methods, and that is that they implicitly assume that other things are equal – for example, that each scientifically meaningful pupil-teacher utterance is of equal importance. A different approach is to focus instead on 'critical incidents'. For example, to examine whether girls and boys obtained equal access to classroom equipment I looked at those rare occasions when equipment was both valued by pupils and in short supply.

Perhaps the most poignant incident of this kind occurred on 16 January and involved Sue, a quiet girl from a working-class background (see p. 43). A Year 8 class were in the library doing a project on astronomy. After watching a video Helen told the class that if they wanted to use the CD-ROM they could only spend 15 minutes on it. At 9.44 a.m. the pupils were allowed to leave their seats and in a rush by some of the pupils Sue got to the CD-ROM first, followed by two boys. Helen then twice called Sue and sent her back to her place on the grounds that she wasn't precise enough about what she wanted to get off the CD-ROM. The two boys were allowed on it instead and were helped by the library assistant. At 9.48 a.m. another boy asked Helen if there was a CD-ROM free. There was, as there were two CD-ROMs in the library, and he asked if he could use it. 'Only if you tell me what you're going to look up on it' said Helen. 'Solar system' said the boy who was then allowed to go onto the free CD-ROM.

At 10.00 a.m. another boy went across and joined the boy who had been working on his own on the CD-ROM. At 10.12 a.m. Helen called across to the four boys on the CD-ROMs 'What about this 15-minute rule?'. One of the boys mumbled something in reply and the four continued to work on the CD-ROMs. At 10.13 a.m. Helen went to look at the work of Sue, congratulated her and gave her a merit. At 10.17 a.m. Sue said to Helen 'When they've finished on that [i.e. either of the CD-ROMs], can I go on and find something about gravity?' Helen agreed and told two of the boys – the ones who had been on the machine since 9.44 a.m. – to come off it, which they did. Sue suggested to another girl that they go on one of the CD-ROMs together which they did at 10.18 a.m. At 10.19 a.m. Helen told the whole class that there were only five minutes left and then told them about their homework and at 10.21 a.m. Sue and the other girl left the CD-ROM as everyone packed up. From 10.23 a.m. Helen clarified what the homework involved and the lesson finished, as usual, at 10.25 a.m.

Hannah Thomson's Special class

Hannah Thomson's Special class contained 24 pupils, 10 of them girls and 14 of them boys. Four of the pupils (Edward, Ian, Jack and Rebecca) had been in the class I had watched in Year 7.

Hannah Thomson had been at Pasmoor School for just one year at the start of Year 8, having arrived as second in the department. Aside from socializing with friends, her major out-of-school interests were sports. She was captain of a successful club hockey team, an avid squash player, adored skiing and also spent time mountaineering and walking.

When I asked her what she was 'trying to achieve in science lessons', Hannah replied:

> This sounds like I'm being interviewed! . . . I'm trying to enthuse pupils about science generally. I'm trying to make them see the relevance of

science to all of them, not just the ones who are going to pursue a scientific career . . . because I try and relate what we're doing . . . my favourite part of a lesson is where they're relating what we're doing to what they've . . . seen on TV . . . at the end of the day my enthusiasm is for science, obviously physics in the main . . . It does my head in really to think of people walking round and not understanding . . . try and get them to think for themselves . . . investigations . . . why and what if . . . [science is] a great subject to teach them planning . . . and [how to be] well organized.

Certainly Hannah's enthusiasm for science came through to me as an observer. Capable of being extremely firm with pupils when the occasion demanded she rarely needed to exert any discipline. When she did, she tended simply to express genuine disappointment at a pupil's behaviour. In the great majority of cases this was quite sufficient to get the pupil working appropriately again. I was intrigued by the fact that the good relationships she established with her class were such that when at one point severe back problems both necessitated her taking time off work and then having a bed in the classroom so that she could lie down when needed, none of the pupils tried to take advantage of this.

Later in the year there was an occasion when Hannah told me during the lesson that she had just had a birthday for which some friends had organized llama trekking as a surprise. At the end of the lesson, at break time, three of the girls in the class came back with some cake for Hannah who, not surprisingly, was genuinely touched, saying 'That's ever so kind of you. I'll get fat!' to which one of the girls cheerfully replied 'That's all right. It'll stop her [pointing at one of the other two] eating all of it!' I left the three girls and Hannah chatting and eating cake.

Hannah was quite prepared to say 'I don't know' on the rare occasions when a pupil asked her a question to which she didn't know the answer, and was perfectly happy to try out, on the spot, a new teaching approach, such as a new way of conducting a revision lesson so as to maintain pupil interest.

James Western's Special class

James Western's Special class contained 25 pupils, 11 of them girls and 14 of them boys. Five of the pupils (Burt, Catherine, Marc, Nicky and Robert) had been in the class I had watched in Year 7.

James Western had been at Pasmoor School about 21 years, his entire teaching career since qualifying. When I asked him about his out-of-school interests, he gave me a long and detailed reply. He had a boat and liked relaxing on the river and fishing. He got involved in arranging the lighting for theatrical productions, telling me that he liked it when a producer would say 'I'd like a dark beam going across there'. He also ran a disco as a business with any profits ploughed back into the business. 'I've always been interested in the whole aspect of making something succeed . . . I need to have something really distractingly challenging to leave this place at weekends and holidays'.

When I asked him what he was 'trying to achieve in science lessons', James replied:

Umm. Big one that [pause] . . . definitely not trying to make kids scientists. I am hoping we'll get them interested in science and consider that as a career, but far more important that it's for all pupils . . . Behind everything there is a practical reality which we want them to get hold of . . . curiosity, questions, develop their understanding of the world . . . it can even help inform beliefs.

At this point we got interrupted by another teacher needing to speak to James briefly. When she had left I repeated that last phrase to him. He told me about a Year 7 teacher:

doing RE [who] starts in the same way as we often start with a Year 11 class – origins of the universe . . . very tied in with people's questions about how did it all start? . . . Why have life? What's the purpose of it? . . . I start Year 7 by asking them what's science about and what makes you different from other animals . . . the search for truth scientifically is very close to the search for God . . . I've had kids ask outright 'Is it true that scientists don't believe in God?' and I say 'Why should there be any conflict between your beliefs and science?'

James had a most distinctive way of teaching. I suppose one could say he constantly strove to get his pupils to mature and to think critically for themselves. To give a flavour of his teaching style, I'll describe, in some detail, the first double lesson I saw him teach. In it the pupils had 50 minutes to finish a study they were doing on soundproofing. James congratulated one girl for bringing in some relevant equipment. One of the boys said 'But we didn't know we were going to do this this week'. James replied 'I said we were going to do it. And if I say something is gonna happen, it happens'. The boy replied 'Yeah, but with most teachers if they say they're going to do something, they don't' to which James rejoined 'Yes, I know, which is why I'm different. I don't like other teachers . . .'

Once the practical work in this lesson began most of the pupils left the lab to conduct their study. I decided to follow Burt and Robert who initially spent some time wandering round the school's corridors asking people if they had a watch with an alarm – a necessary piece of equipment for their study. No one, including me, did. After some debate, Burt and Robert summoned up the courage to go into a lesson Stephen Benton was teaching to ask one particular pupil if he had a watch with an alarm. Before they went in they asked me if I thought it would be safe to do so. I said that I would tell them after they had tried it and waited outside as they went into the lesson.

Stephen Benton got annoyed with them for interrupting his lesson and told them to ask a lab technician and 'stop wasting my time'. Retreating from Stephen's lab, Burt looked shell-shocked for some half a minute at this turn of events and I helpfully told the two of them that I didn't think it would be safe going into Stephen's lesson. 'Thanks a lot' replied Burt.

Eventually Burt and Robert succeeded in obtaining a stopwatch from a technician, only to find that neither of them could get it to work. 'Not a very good start to the day' remarked Burt to which I, who was rather enjoying the Kafkaesque feel to the proceedings, replied 'How do you know? This might be the highlight of the year. You might spend the rest of your life wandering around school corridors'.

Burt, understandably, got frustrated at not being able to get the alarm of the stopwatch to work. They needed it to because their experimental design involved them surrounding it with different sound-insulating materials so that they could determine from how far away they could still hear the noise. Robert, with his perennial, placid approach to life waited calmly with me while Burt headed off to James Western to find out how the alarm on the stopwatch worked. He returned to the two of us a minute later saying 'He doesn't know, either'. Burt then handed the stopwatch to me and I spent three minutes failing to get its alarm to work (so much for non-participant observation).

The three of us drifted back to the lesson some 19 minutes after we had left it and Robert succeeded in getting one of the alarm clocks in the lab to work even though James had earlier told them that they had been disabled 'because kids play around with them'. After overcoming further difficulties Burt and Robert eventually succeeded in getting their required readings in one of the corridors with a variety of sound-insulating materials. At one point James himself found the two of them and checked they were getting on OK.

Burt and Robert returned to the classroom at 9.55 a.m. just in time for James to start telling the 15 members of the class present rather than still roaming the school's corridors about what they would be doing in the next double lesson. (All 25 members of the class were present at the start of the lesson.) He wanted them to design and make a musical instrument and encouraged them to think about how they would vary the frequency of the sound, tune their instrument, make sure it could be heard and so forth. He concluded: 'It's not plan it, do it, judge it, 'cos life isn't like that. It's plan it, do it, goes wrong, redo it, goes wrong, redesign it. 'Cos life goes round in circles'.

At this point, 10.00 a.m., five more pupils returned and James gave them a brief overview of what he had been saying for the last five minutes. The pupils then started to design their musical instruments. James mostly spent the next 15 minutes going round talking to pupils about their ideas but found time to come across to me for a minute. He said to me that it must be nice for me to see a lesson such as this where the pupils are in control rather than 'a very structured one where they all do the same for 20 minutes and you end up writing that they haven't done anything'. I said that it was nice for me to have been able to follow Burt and Robert for 50 minutes and really see what they were doing. By now all 25 pupils were present again.

Table 3.1   Questions asked by me of the parents of the Year 8 pupils

1(a) How do you think [your child] has got on this last year at Pasmoor School?
1(b) [As 1a but specifically in science].
2(a) Could you [parent 1] tell me a bit about your education, please?
2(b) Could you [parent 2] tell me a bit about your education, please?
3   Do you think science should be taught to all children in schools? Could you say why, please?
4   What do you understand by the word 'science'?
5   What do you think scientists spend their time doing?

At 10.15 a.m. I noted that Catherine had been sitting with her head in her arms. Indeed, she had looked pretty dozy/dreamy for most of the lesson. Just at that point she suddenly sprang to life when an older boy appeared at the door with something. Catherine, Nicky and another female pupil disappeared with him at 10.16 a.m.

At 10.16 a.m. James quietened down the remaining 22 pupils and emphasized that he was showing a lot of trust in them. 'I do want to give you some space, some time. I don't want you to do music. I do want you to do science. The two of them are very closely related though you may think of music as an arts subject'. James told them that he didn't just want them to copy a musical instrument they knew. Indeed, next time he'd like them to be able to explain the principles of their instrument to the rest of the group. He told them that by a week from now they should have shown their instrument to 'friends and parents and someone up the street' to have really improved it.

At 10.25 a.m. the hooter went and the class was dismissed. Catherine, Nicky and the other female pupil had not returned and other girls packed up for them.

Parents' experiences of their own science education

At the end of year interview (see Table 3.1), I asked parents about their own educational background, what their own experiences of science lessons at school had been and whether they thought science should be taught to all pupils. There were a number of reasons why I asked these questions. For a start I was simply interested in seeing how the parents had experienced their schooling in general and science eduation in particular. I was also interested in the general question as to whether there was a relationship between home background and what the pupils eventually chose to do on leaving Pasmoor School. This question is examined later (see p. 153). One more immediate issue, which I explore here, is whether there is any relationship between parents' own experiences of school science and whether they think it should be a compulsory subject.

To help organize these accounts I have divided the parents up into four 'blocks', each block corresponding to the class in which their daughter or son was for Year 8 science, beginning with the Foundation class and going through to the two Special classes. Within each of these four blocks, parents are listed by alphabetical order of their daughter/son's pseudonym.

The parents of George, Peter and Rodney

George's mother 'never had any interest in science whatsoever'. She went to an 11–16 school and did no science O levels, doing geography O level instead. She did English and sociology A levels. Having passed these she got a job. At the time of interview she was working part-time in a bank.

George's father always knew that he was going to be a farmer. His own father had farmed the same farm before him. George's father had been to Pasmoor School. ''Cos I knew I was going to be a farmer, I didn't try all that hard'. He did seven CSEs, including physics. He also did biology O level 'and failed it but still did better than some of the bright sparks', which he was clearly chuffed about. 'I liked chemistry but I'd already elected to do physics and biology'. Afterwards he did four years of day release at a local agricultural college and got five City & Guilds.

Peter's mother 'went to quite a few schools because we moved around. I went to some excellent ones and some terrible ones'. She had stopped doing science before she did her CSEs. 'All I remember is Bunsen burners and test-tubes and being fined 5p'. The fine was for breaking some science equipment. They used to do dissection in biology and she found that 'horrible . . . Also had to go out and collect snails and collect worms and make a wormery and my Mum was disgusted'. After leaving school she went and worked in a hospital but she did her back in so had to leave after eight months. Since then she had worked in retail and at the time of interview was a manager.

After infant and junior schools Peter's stepfather had gone to a secondary modern. He had dropped science before doing his GCSEs. After leaving school he joined a building firm as a carpenter/joiner and then spent five years doing City & Guilds and construction technology. At the time of interview he was an inspector with a big window company.

Rodney's mother failed the 11+, having been off school for almost a year on account of bronchitis. She then did two years at a secondary modern and then under the Mason scheme, which, as I told her, I had never heard of, went to a grammar school. The teachers at the school didn't approve of the Mason scheme and so 'refused to teach us . . . I was the only one in the set who didn't get five O levels'. She then trained to be a nurse and went into nursing. She hadn't many memories of her science education. 'I enjoyed the chemistry lessons and biology, of course'.

Rodney's mother told me that her husband had wanted to be an architect but various difficulties had meant that he had ended up doing surveying instead. At the time of interview he worked in business.

The parents of Martin, Mary, Paul, Richard and Sue

Martin's mother had gone to a secondary modern. She did O levels in maths, English language and needlework and CSEs in commerce, typing, banking and accounts. She didn't do any science in her last year at school; before that she had done chemistry, biology and general science. She left school at 16 and got a job at the steelworks. She did typing but didn't like it. She then did a couple of RSAs, then hairdressing and at the time of interview worked in the food hall of a major retailer.

Martin's father had grown up on a working farm: 'there was a lot of money spent on my education and I wasted it. Basically I was not interested in anything else except working on the farm and playing cricket'. He got O levels in English language and English literature and did the O level in chemistry & physics. He left school at the age of 16 and sat or resat maths and agricultural science and got them. He did City & Guilds on day release at technical college for three years and then the farm 'went bust . . . and at that point you think, bloody hell, I wish I'd done more at school'. I asked what it was like when the farm went bust. 'Twenty-six years ago and I can remember my old man calling in my brother and me one Sunday evening and telling us . . . it was the time of foot-and-mouth. No money in for a year . . . c'est la vie.' For the last 12 years he had worked for an agricultural company, driving and doing warehouse duties, etc.

Mary's mother went to a state Catholic primary school and then had a year in another school 'when I realized I was a long way behind. I was right at the bottom'. Thanks to one teacher she passed her 11+ and went to a convent grammar school where she boarded. She did biology O level and enjoyed it but never grasped physics and chemistry. After O levels she went into the sixth form. She wanted to go to a teacher training college but the school 'would only give you a reference if you went to a Catholic college. My parents thought this wasn't fair'. As a result they removed her from the school and sent her to another one. The trouble was this meant that her A levels changed from English, French and history to English, French and art. Not only that but she had all the problems associated with different set books in English. Her mother was also unwell and she ended up with no A levels. She went to college and got a General Teaching Certificate (primary and nursing). She did a year to enable her to teach hearing-impaired children. Subsequent to that she did an Open University degree during which her then husband died, six weeks before Mary was born. More recently still she completed a course in personnel management. At the time of interview she was a part-time peripatetic teacher of the deaf.

Mary's father had done four science A levels and then went to university to read electrical engineering. However, he had failed the first year so he got a job and did day release. He then did an MSc and was a scientist.

Mary's stepfather had gone to primary school in Scotland and then to grammar school in England. He did eight O levels including 'a combined physics/chemistry O level. I don't remember doing biology . . . I've never been that interested in science'. He then did A levels in English, Latin, another language and general studies followed by a law degree. He qualified as a solicitor and at the time of interview worked for a county council as a solicitor.

Paul's mother initially replied 'Don't bother with me. Not worth it'. The school she went to was for 'the 11+ failures . . . There was no intake for a year because they weren't sure whether to close us'. All pupils 'had to do chemistry and biology or physics and chemistry. I did chemistry and biology. I couldn't understand chemistry. If I'd been allowed to do physics I would have understood it . . . the chemistry teacher hated me and said in front of me "She came from a council estate so what can you expect"'. She told me that they 'all failed biology because they put us in for the wrong syllabus'. She had stayed on at school until the age of 17 to do O levels and then successfully trained as a nurse and went into nursing.

Paul's father had been to a secondary modern. He had been good at biology but 'had a pretty useless science teacher . . . used to like it but always had the fear of being told off . . . All I can remember is magnets and fulcrum and drawing a Bunsen burner'. He had stayed on half a year at school and done RSAs. Then he went into further education and got an O level in maths. He then joined the civil service and did a correspondence course. He had just moved jobs and was working in the Employment Department in London.

Richard's mother told me that ''Cos my dad was in the forces I must have had at least six schools'. She said she 'enjoyed most lessons' but 'I was awful at science . . . 'cos I didn't want to dissect I didn't do biology so I did physics and chemistry and didn't understand either!' She left school at 15 and went to a college of arts and technology where she did five O levels, none of which were science. She then did a secretarial course and went to work at 17. At the time of interview she was still a secretary.

Richard's father was in the last year when one could leave school at 15. He stayed on and did five CSEs including physics, having had a choice of chemistry or physics. He then did a year at college where he did O levels in maths and technical drawing. Then he joined the telecommunications side of the Post Office as an apprentice. He did 'all the City & Guilds telecommunications courses . . . on valves, magnetism . . . took five years. I went all the .way through. Got the full certificate . . . Then I had a pause. Then I started doing HNC business studies, then diploma in management studies, then diploma in marketing . . . currently enrolled to do an MSc in business systems management'. After working for what became BT for 23 years, at the time of interview he worked for the county council in charge of reorganizing one of their departments.

Sue's mother had been to Pasmoor School too. Her memory of science was 'Bunsen burners'. She had left at the age of 15 and gone to work.

Sue's father had been put in the remedial group in his first year at secondary school. His was the first year you had to stay on till 16 and he had got CSEs in typing and technical drawing. He had also enjoyed drama but it had been cancelled after the first year of the CSE because there weren't enough pupils in the set. He had done basic science and told me that he enjoyed tampering with TVs. He recounted how he had recently bought a video machine from a car boot sale for a fiver because it had a 'problem and within two minutes had it working'. At the time of interview he worked as a driver.

The parents of Edward, Ian, Jack and Rebecca

Edward's mother had been to a Church of England primary school and then a secondary school 'where unfortunately there was more bias towards CSEs than O levels'. She had a 'wonderful human biology teacher' and got a CSE Grade 1 in that. However, her 'physics and chemistry teachers were grim'. She had done A levels in history of art and English and then went to college and trained as a nurse. As her husband pointed out 'a lot of that to do with things that had a scientific basis'. She had done nursery nursing and dental nursing and at the time of interview was principal of a nursery school.

Edward's father remembered the space race being of great interest to him as he grew up. After primary school he had gone to a boys' grammar school. When he was about 14 or 15 there was a chemistry class with 'quite a lot of disruption. The teacher said "All those who want to do chemistry sit up the front; the rest of you sit at the back". I sat in the middle so that rather dented my chemistry'. He remembered really good physics teachers and enjoying the experiments. He also did biology O level and passed that. He did physics and Maths A levels but didn't pass them. At this point his wife told me that he had had glandular fever at this time. He then went to college and did A levels in English and psychology. After a year as a bank clerk he 'stumbled into computing and have always maintained an interest not in chemistry but in general science . . . occasionally buy *New Scientist* and watch *Tomorrow's World*'. At the time of interview he was still in computing and ran his own company.

Ian's mother had dropped science after two years at secondary school 'and feel a bit frustrated because I watch *Horizon* and think "Wow, I haven't even got the language". I rely on my husband for the science because I feel I haven't got the knowledge'. She had done a degree in French and industrial relations and was now a primary teacher. 'I teach primary science which I enjoy . . . there comes a cut-off point with jargon . . . at the minute, primary science makes it seem much more accessible and much less "you can or you can't"'.

Ian's mother said of her husband 'Well, he's completely science . . . His degree is in astronomy. He did physics and maths at A level. Did an MSc in astronomy . . . He works in research and development in computer graphics in a Cambridge company'.

Jack's mother described herself as having had a 'total lack of any science education at all'. She had been to a private day primary school and then to two very small girls' private boarding schools. Biology was taught in the second one, and she had done her O levels, including biology, at the age of 14.

She remembered dissecting buttercups and the growth of broad beans and had enjoyed biology. She had then done A levels in English and British constitution at the age of 15. She looked back at her school education 'with sadness'. She had had 'no real maths teaching till age 14 . . . Did get taught how to curtsy! . . . Very poor English teaching'. After school she had done a secretarial course and worked as a secretary at Oxfam and then gone to further education and done English and history A levels. This had been followed by a degree in English. She had recently started a job in the restoration unit at a museum having had to give up her previous job when the family moved to their present home in August 1994. This was because the firm her husband worked for had been taken over and he had been relocated.

Jack's father had been to a prep school at which he had been very unhappy and then to a second prep school at which he had been very happy. After those he went to a leading independent school. His mother had died when he was 14 and at 15 he had had to choose between music and science. He did his A levels in pure maths, applied maths and physical science but felt that he had been pushed towards doing the two maths A levels by his father. He read physics at university which he felt was 'a mistake. I should have read engineering'. He then got a job and then did a PhD. At the time of interview he worked as a research geophysicist at a major international company with one of its research units at Cambridge.

Rebecca's mother had gone to a single-sex grammar school. At the age of 13 she had had to choose between doing biology O level and physics with chemistry O level or doing separate chemistry and physics O levels. She chose the latter. I commented that it was unusual at that time for a girl to do chemistry and physics but not biology. She told me that she enjoyed the chemistry more than biology, liking 'things that went bang, pretty colours, things that grew' (i.e. crystals). She then went to university to do social sciences but dropped out after a term. Purely by accident she ended up working with people with physical disabilities and the elderly. She then did a City & Guilds advanced management in care and then a diploma in social work. At the time of interview she was managing an old people's home.

Rebecca's father had been educated in Canada. He had done biology, chemistry and physics through to Grade 13. He had 'enjoyed science . . . still remember dissecting frogs'. Having come over to the UK he joined Customs and Excise. He got a diploma in management studies and at the time of interview was doing an MSc.

The parents of Burt, Catherine, Marc, Nicky and Robert

Burt's mother had gone to a convent school where she took eight O levels and then got two A levels elsewhere. She did an external degree in history and taught in primary schools, doing a PGCE *en route*. She thought she had done biology O level but the school didn't really do physics and chemistry because it was a girls' school.

Burt's father was in the home but it was clear he didn't want to be interviewed. Burt's mother told me that, after O and A levels, he had gone to university and studied economics, theology and law. At that time he was a solicitor.

Catherine's mother had passed her 11+ and gone to grammar school. There she did a general science course which counted as a single O level. She had had three different teachers for it, one for biology, one for chemistry and one for physics. She left school at 16. After having done a year's unqualified teaching she went to teacher training college. She specialized in RE with primary science as a subsidiary course. At the time of interview she was a primary head teacher.

Catherine's mother told me that her husband had gone to the same grammar school and had taken the same general science course as she. He had gone into the sixth form but left during the first year to be an articled clerk to a firm of accountants. He then did a correspondence course over five years and qualified as a chartered accountant. At the time of interview this was still his profession.

Marc's mother had moved around 'quite a bit because of family circumstances . . . I think I went to four [primary schools] and moved secondary after two years . . . Then I went to the old grammar school; then to two schools near . . . and I fluffed my exams and went to the tech for a year'. She had done O levels and CSEs but didn't take A levels. Then she trained to be a home economics teacher. She said that she 'gave up science in the third year [at secondary school] . . . home economics not classified as a science'. She had gone into teaching and had been an under-8s adviser.

Marc's mother didn't know much about Marc's father's education though she knew he didn't go to college.

Marc's stepfather remembered reading from the age of $2^1/_2$. He had been to a Roman Catholic primary school: 'that's where my love of history came from and that's where my potential for science was squished'. He had then gone to a middle school and then to a comprehensive. He did eight O levels and three CSEs, all at Grade 1. He had done chemistry and physics but 'I didn't take biology, took geography instead, thank goodness, cutting things up didn't appeal'. He said quite a bit more about not wanting to do dissection. He stayed on at the school and had wanted to do four A levels of which physics would have been one. However, the timetable wouldn't allow it so he took English, history, economics and general studies. He then half remembered a quote about 'It's all physics; the rest is stamp collecting'. I asked him how he felt about that and he said 'It's pretty close to the mark'. After a degree in history and politics he did a PGCE in history and English and then taught for seven years at a comprehensive and at a sixth-form college. At the time of interview he was self-employed, working in the field of personality development and neurolinguistic programming.

Nicky's mother 'went to the girls' grammar school and didn't enjoy science very much at all . . . I enjoyed the biology side but not the physics or the chemistry'. She had done biology, chemistry and physics O levels, passing biology but not the other two. After leaving school 'I went to work in an office'.

Nicky's father had gone to an 11–16 comprehensive. 'I thoroughly enjoyed chemistry; chemistry and physics but not the biology so much . . .' He had done a blend of O levels and CSEs including O level physics and CSE chemistry. Although his brothers went to university, 'I'd had enough of education; teachers put me off' so he left school at 16 and went to work at a local technology company. Here he did day release and an ONC and HNC in electronics. He was still with the same company. At the time of interview he worked installing one-off automated chromatography systems, often for the petrochemical industry. He spent about 100 days a year abroad doing this.

Robert's mother described her education as 'Total failure basically'. After primary school she too had gone to Pasmoor School. 'I just gave up and they let me. I went to school. I didn't hate going. None of the teachers ever pestered me. I never did any homework and I was never chased up about it, not once that I can remember'. She now wished that someone at school had pushed her. In fact, on my first visit in Year 7 she had told me that she had always come bottom of the class in everything. When she had gone to Pasmoor School she was put in a 'special class'. However, they didn't provide much real extra help and at the end of the year when she went back into the normal class it was worse than if she had never been in the special class because she had missed out on everything the normal classes had done in the first year. 'I cannot spell and punctuate . . . I can never remember being taught about full stops . . .' At the time of interview she worked at a college with special needs students. She helped them cook and, with a certain irony which she appreciated, 'I sometimes have to help them write'.

Robert's father, after leaving primary school, went to a comprehensive. In the third year the boys did physics and the girls did biology. His O level grades were better than expected and included O level physics. He then did an O level in engineering science which was a 'bit of a waste of time . . . Then I just went out to work and no one ever asked what my O levels were'. At the time of interview he ran his own business.

Comment on parental experiences of their own science education

I found these brief educational biographies moving. I noted both the extent to which many of the parents had suffered significant disruptions to their schooling, for one reason or another, and the degree to which many of them had continued with their education after leaving full-time education.

As far as their science education went it was rather disheartening to me as a science educator to hear how many of them had had fairly negative experiences of school science. It was also noteworthy how few of them had had what would nowadays be termed a 'balanced science education'. Since the introduction of the National Curriculum in 1989 virtually all pupils in England and Wales have studied science continuously from the age of 5 through to 16. In addition, the science they study contains equal amounts of biology, chemistry and physics, together with some astronomy and Earth sciences. Around 90 per cent of 16-year-olds in England and Wales take either two or three GCSEs in science. Most of the remaining 10 per cent take a single science GCSE.

Should science be taught to all pupils in schools?

Of the 29 parents asked 'Do you think science should be taught to all children in schools?', 25 replied 'Yes', 'Definitely' or 'Most certainly'. Although Marc's stepfather said 'Yes' he added:

> But why label it 'science'? To many people the very label has an impact upon parents' perceptions and that's passed on to children . . . preconceived science is difficult when actually it's the easiest thing in the world . . . I'm a bit of an iconoclast because I believe children should be taught how to learn rather than the content of particular subjects . . . I believe teachers in teacher training should be taught how to enable children to learn and not how to teach their subject and I think people in teacher training need to be better . . . things like accelerated learning techniques . . . mind mapping . . . neurolinguistic programming . . .

In addition to the 25 parents who replied 'Yes', 'Definitely' or 'Most certainly', George's father replied 'Umm, I would say probably yes' and Martin's father replied 'Probably yes'. Rodney's mother was more ambivalent replying 'Yes, definitely; well I don't know . . . I see no point in teaching physics to a kid who's not capable of grasping it because it'll just humiliate them'. Martin's mother explained how she had enjoyed biology but added 'I didn't like the experiments. Unless you're going into work with science there's not much point in it'.

When I asked the parents why they felt as they did about whether science should be taught to all pupils in schools, I was able to classify their answers into five categories, as listed below.

Deepen one's understanding

> Science is life really. It's everything around us. It's important to give children a chance to look deeply into natural science as well as all the other scientific areas.
>
> (Catherine's mother)

> It's a basic part of understanding the world we live in.
>
> (Edward's father)

> I think it's very noticeable that when you meet people who don't have any science, they don't realize how much they don't know.
>
> (Jack's father)

I think it's nice to know how everything functions in your body.

(Martin's mother)

I certainly think they should be taught how the world works.

(Martin's father)

We live in such a technological age.

(Mary's mother)

So they can understand everyday things, the weather, the reason the TV goes on and off.

(Paul's mother)

I think it's nice for them to know how things tick, like circuits

(Peter's mother)

For example, if you see a fence, having studied science you know that it is made of wood and molecules.

(Rebecca's father)

It's relevant to lots of things.

(Robert's mother)

To me personally, life is science; life is a learning process.

(Sue's father)

Part of a balanced education

Children should have an all-round education.

(Catherine's mother)

I don't think children know what they're interested in till they try it.

(George's father)

I think it's this access thing and memories of there being a cut-off point in the past.

(Ian's mother)

It's part of an all-round education.

(Mary's stepfather)

'Cos I think it comes into all sorts of different courses.

(Nicky's mother)

I think children should be taught as wide a range of subjects as possible.

(Rebecca's mother)

'Cos it underpins all other subjects.

(Richard's father)

Valuable for employment

> It's the analytical way of thinking that's very important in functioning in the real world in a lot of jobs.
>
> (Edward's father)

> A degree in arts doesn't exactly lead to a fortune.
>
> (Ian's mother)

> I know how I struggled without it when I came to something I wanted to do [i.e. train as a home economics teacher].
>
> (Marc's mother)

Interesting

> Getting an interest early on.
>
> (Edward's mother)

> I think it's incredibly interesting and I'm sorry that I missed out on it and I think children find it naturally interesting.
>
> (Jack's mother)

Other

> I suppose to have more logical questioning attitudes.
>
> (Burt's mother)

> Helps them to explore investigations and how things happen.
>
> (Paul's father)

Comment on parents' views as to whether science should be taught to all pupils and if so, why

Despite the diversity of experiences parents had had of school science, including some quite negative experiences, there was near universal parental support for the idea that science should be taught to all pupils in schools. While the categories into which their reasons fell overlap to some extent, the most common reason given was because a science education would help children's understanding in some way. The next most common reason was that a science education is part of a balanced education.

It is clear that there is exceptionally strong support from parents for science being taught to all pupils in schools. I admit that I was somewhat surprised at this. It is possible that the fact that the parents knew that I was involved in science education might have caused some of them to be more positive about science than would otherwise have been the case. However, a 1998/9 study of 117 parents in focus groups also found that:

All parents expressed the view that science, which was seen to include aspects of technology, was one of the most important subjects for their children to study at school. The principal reason was the need for young people to gain an understanding of the world in which they live and of the socio-scientific issues which affect their lives.

(Osborne and Collins 1999: 15)

Key points

- On entering Year 8 the pupils in the one class I had followed in Year 7 were divided into four classes, differentiated by ability.
- The four science teachers I observed in Year 8 had distinct philosophies about science education and very different ways of teaching science.
- Some help was provided by learning support assistants for certain pupils.
- Many of the parents of the pupils I was following had had rather negative experiences of school science in their own education.
- Parents were overwhelmingly supportive of the notion that school science was important and should be compulsory for all pupils.

4

Year 9: 'What's a slag, Mr Western?'

There were a range of orientations to the official curriculum and
varying degrees of cultural investment in creating informal leisure
spaces.

(Mac an Ghaill 1994: 137)

The background to Year 9

On their return to school for the start of Year 9 the pupils I was following were
arranged in four classes, as in Year 8. The principal difference from Year 8 was
that each class now had two teachers, one who covered biology and some
chemistry, the other who covered physics and some chemistry. As in Year 8,
two of the classes were described as Special classes and one as a Merit class.
However, the Foundation class was now described as a Credit class.

As in Chapter 3, part of my aim here is to give a real flavour of what life was
like for the pupils in these classes. I became convinced that one of the
strongest influences on this was the characteristics of the various teachers –
their personalities and classroom performances. For this reason I spend some
time below describing lessons and the teaching philosophy of the three
teachers not described in Chapter 3. It is worth mentioning that all the pupils
I was following had new science teachers in Year 9 compared with those they
had had in Year 7 and Year 8. Most of them, though, remained in classes with
much the same pupil composition. Only Martin (down) and Mary (up)
moved sets between Year 8 and Year 9.

At the end of the Year 9 interviews I collected in exercise books from those
pupils who could find them at home. By describing the ways teachers
responded to the work in these exercise books and by including a sample of
each pupil's work I hope to give more of a feel of how each pupil was performing in the science lessons.

Roland Newman's and James Western's Credit class

The Credit class that Roland Newman and James Western shared had just 12 pupils – 3 girls and 9 boys. It contained four of the pupils I was following (George, Martin, Peter and Rodney). Martin had therefore been moved down a set from Year 8. Roland Newman taught the biology and some of the chemistry; James Western the physics and some of the chemistry.

Roland Newman's teaching

Roland had been at Pasmoor School for seven years and was the head of the science department. Outside of school he did a lot of rugby refereeing at quite a senior level as well as walking, cycling, going to the cinema and travelling. He wanted his science lessons to provide 'A combination of excitement and interest, and supporting pupils to achieve the best they can in a lesson, and relevance . . . as relevant as possible in their lives'.

Both Roland and James expected high standards of work from the pupils in the Credit class. As I provided a description of one of James' lessons earlier (see pp. 55–7), I'll describe one of Roland's here. In fact, I saw comparatively few lessons taught by Roland during Year 9 as during both the autumn and spring terms there were a number of student teachers teaching part or all of his Year 9 Credit and Special classes that I was observing. The double lesson described here was on 11 April (a Friday afternoon – not the most popular time for most teachers to be teaching a 'bottom' set), at the start of the summer term. A learning support assistant, Bernadette McLaughlin, was also present.

At the beginning of the lesson, Roland gathered the 12 pupils round the front and had a question and answer session with them about photosynthesis. He then introduced a practical on photosynthesis in pondweed by telling them 'Now. We've got a problem 'cos this doesn't always work, so it's a test of your patience. I can't always guarantee your results'. He explained that it was a bit early in the year for pondweed, so they ought to go for the greenest pondweed possible.

Roland then added a powder to the water (presumably sodium hydrogen carbonate or suchlike) and one of the boys said that this would give off carbon dioxide. Roland was impressed with this statement and told the boy so. Another boy then said that the powder would give off food and Roland explained that it wasn't food that would be given off, just carbon dioxide.

Roland then demonstrated the method, which entailed counting the bubbles of gas given off by the photosynthesizing plant. One of the boys suggested shining a light. Roland agreed with this suggestion and got the boy to explain why this would be a good idea. Roland told them that it would take a while for bubbles to start appearing and asked them why they thought this was. One of the girls and Rodney contributed suggestions.

Roland told them to carry out the experiment with three different distances between the lamp and the plant: 5cm, 10cm and 30cm. They should get three sets of readings, each over the course of one minute, at each distance and wait five minutes before taking any readings at a new distance. George suggested that if they kept the distance the same rather than increasing it, the bubbles would come off faster and faster. Roland suggested that George's group could test this while the other groups investigated the effect of distance.

Rodney then said that the practical might not be a fair test because the bulbs might be of different strengths. Roland asked if that would matter if they used the same lamp within their group. Rodney said it would matter if they wanted to combine their results (i.e. from different groups). Roland agreed. Rodney then said that the water might get warmed up by the light. Roland said that this was a really good point and that he would get some thermometers.

At 1.39 p.m., the lesson having started at 1.10 p.m. the pupils started their experiments, working in twos or threes. Roland and Bernadette then went round the groups helping and encouraging. At one point Roland came and chatted with me for three minutes. He commented on how this group could come out with really good scientific comments – mentioning the possibility raised by Rodney of the lamp heating the water – but that the problem was one of concentration span.

At 2.32 p.m., Roland quietened the whole group and got everyone to switch off their lamps and bring their books, with their results in, up to the front bench. He then collated their results on the board and spent 11 minutes getting the pupils to talk about their results and the pattern they had found. Just about everyone joined in this discussion. For example, when, contrary to other groups, Martin and the boy with whom he was working found that more bubbles were given off as the distance between the lamp and the pondweed increased, Peter suggested why this might be, as did one of the girls and then Rodney too.

The last seven minutes were spent clearing up apparatus, writing down what the homework was, packing up bags and putting chairs up for the end of the day. At 2.50 p.m. the hooter went for the end of the day and Roland, after quietening the class, congratulated them, as he often did, on their work and dismissed them.

Pupils' exercise books

Martin received lots of positive comments in his exercise book: 'V good neat work', 'Good work Martin, Merit' and 'Ex. Well done', for example. His write-up of pressure is shown in Figure 4.1.

George couldn't find either of his Year 9 books (though he did still have his exercise books from Year 7 and Year 8).

Peter's comments were variable: 'Pencil diagrams please Peter', 'A good homework Peter', 'You can produce some good work Peter, if only you settle and concentrate in class. Where is your homework?' and 'You need to copy

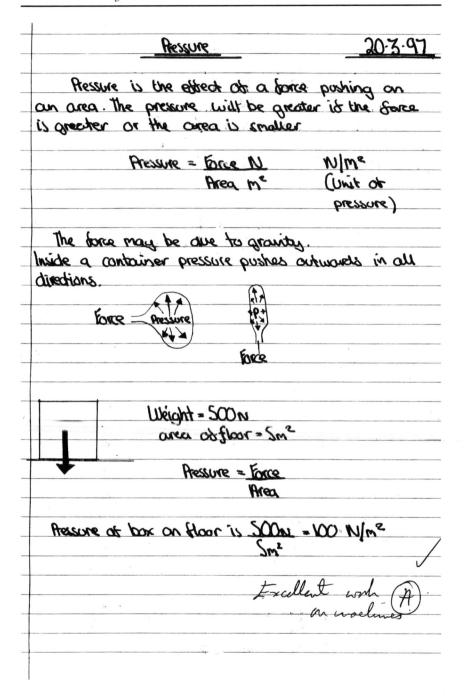

Figure 4.1 An example of Martin's work

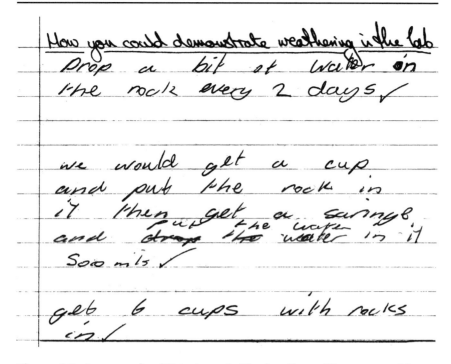

Figure 4.2 An example of Peter's work. The heading – 'How you could demonstrate weathering in the lab' – was provided by the teacher, Roland Newman

up the work you have missed Peter', for example. A sample of Peter's work is shown in Figure 4.2, where the teacher, Roland, has written in the heading when marking the work.

Rodney's comments were variable: 'Homework missing. See me', 'Good diagrams Rodney', 'Good classwork Rodney', 'Do not forget to copy up the work you missed' and 'You can do good work when you concentrate', for example. A sample of his writing is shown in Figure 4.3.

Susan de Von's and Katie Toland's Merit class

The Merit class that Susan de Von and Katie Toland taught had 20 pupils, seven of them girls and 13 of them boys. The class contained three of the pupils I was especially interested in (Paul, Richard and Sue). Susan de Von taught the physics and some of the chemistry. Katie Toland taught the biology and some of the chemistry.

Photosynthesis

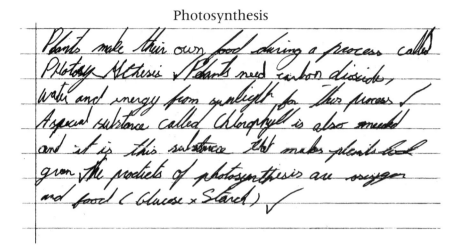

Figure 4.3   One of Rodney's more complete pieces of work

Susan de Von's teaching

Susan was now in her sixth year at Pasmoor School and was assistant head of year, subsequently becoming head of year. Outside of school her priorities were the family with her two young children. She told me she was 'also quite keen on sport . . . aerobics and things like that . . . netball'. She liked to teach science 'From a sort of practical hands-on start, really. And, nothing special really, nothing original; to link it to real outside experience as much as possible and to get them to question, really'.

In the classroom Susan expected, and got, pupils to pay attention and work hard. At the same time she loved making occasional off-the-cuff humorous remarks which I and many in the class greatly appreciated. Frequently this humour was used as a gentle, but highly effective, way of telling a pupil to get back to doing the science.

As an illustration of Susan's teaching (pulled at random from my notes as was Roland's above) I'll describe a double lesson on the afternoon of 14 March. This was 'Red Nose Day' so the pupils were not in school uniform and at the beginning of the lesson were quite excited as one of the teachers had been 'gunged' (to raise money for charity) at lunchtime, just before this lesson.

One of the boys spent the first 50 minutes (1.10 to 2.00 p.m.) in a corner of the lab doing the end-of-topic test on electrical circuits he had previously missed. Having sorted this out, Susan then began the main part of the lesson by telling the rest of the class that they were about to start the new topic 'Particle world' by watching a video. She drew the blinds, gathered the pupils round the video, told them that some of them (but not all of them) would have seen the video before and turned it on.

The video lasted 20 minutes from 1.25 p.m. to 1.45 p.m. Susan then got the blinds raised and started a demonstration with the pupils still gathered round the front. She had a kettle beginning to boil and used it to ask them how they would decide if something was a solid. One girl said if it's hard; another girl said if it goes through a sieve (this was on the video). After a contribution from one of the boys Susan talked about how it is sometimes quite difficult to decide whether something is a solid. She asked them what a solid keeps and one of the boys said what she wanted – 'its shape'. Another boy contributed something and then Susan asked Sue how you can see if something is a gas. Sue was hesitant and Susan helped her by asking 'Does it keep its shape?' Sue answered no and Susan agreed with her.

Susan told one of the boys to sit up and another boy asked a question, dis-agreeing that solids keep their shape. Another boy said that if the kettle wasn't full, the steam wouldn't, when the kettle boiled, fill the whole room. Susan explained how the steam could end up anywhere in the room and explained that the same thing, for example, is true about perfume.

One of the girls had had hiccups for the last five minutes and Susan sug-gested she went and got a drink of water, which she did, returning soon after. Susan led the discussion onto an explicit consideration of particles. She got one of the boys to say that in a solid the particles are close together. Susan then asked them what they thought would happen to the particles in a solid if the solid warmed up. No one volunteered. She asked Richard and gave him a hint, telling him that the particles were moving about a little and asking what they would do more. Richard got it right and Susan went on to talk about liquids and gases with contributions from several boys.

At 1.58 p.m. Susan got pupils to get a textbook each from the side and turn to a particular page. She then asked for a volunteer to read. One of the girls volunteered and read about the particle model of matter. Once the girl had finished reading Susan talked about what she had read. At 2.01 p.m. the pupils returned to their seats to copy out some diagrams and do some writing. Soon afterwards the boy who had spent the first half of the double lesson doing the test asked Susan if she would be able to mark his test today. Smil-ing she said: 'If I've got five hands'. The boy grinned and Susan added 'I'll try'.

Susan then started setting up a demonstration on the front bench. It was one I remembered well as it was, I think, the first bit of science I did when I moved to my new school at the age of 13. Interestingly, what I now remem-ber, almost 30 years later, is the teacher setting the demonstration up and the drawing I did in my exercise book of the demonstration, rather than the demonstration itself. The demonstration was of the diffusion of ammonia vapour and hydrochloric acid vapour along a long, thin glass tube from oppo-site ends.

At 2.13 p.m., while the pupils were still working quietly, one of the girls suddenly announced 'I thought of something to say last night but I can't remember it now'. One of the boys commented 'She's always saying that' and another boy cheerfully asked Susan 'Can we gag her?' 'We'd need quite a few gags in this classroom' replied Susan. After a minute's quiet the same girl said something else non-scientific to her neighbour and Susan said, more firmly '[the girl's name], can we give it a rest, please?'

By 2.19 p.m. several pupils had finished their copying out and Susan told the whole class that they had just two minutes more. By now Susan had finished setting up the demonstration and had been discussing particles with individual pupils.

At 2.21 p.m. Susan gathered the pupils round the front. She quietened them and put on a pair of goggles herself. She told them that she was going to put cotton wool soaked in ammonia in one and cotton wool soaked in very concentrated hydrochloric acid at the other end of the horizontal glass tube. She got one of the boys to open the windows and another boy regaled the class with uplifting accounts of a Newcastle footballer who got ammonia sprayed in his eyes. One girl got muddled between pneumonia and ammonia and was derided by some in the class.

At 2.25 p.m. Susan had the apparatus fully set up and was coughing a bit because of the fumes. She then got pupils to think about what might happen in the demonstration. There was a strip of litmus paper along the tube – something I don't remember from my own schooldays – and one of the boys commented that it was changing colour. Another boy said that this was because gas was moving along. Another boy added that one side was alkali and the other side was acid. One boy said that they were not travelling at the same speed. Richard said that the two gases might meet up. Susan asked what happens when acidic substances meet with alkali substances, adding 'I'd like every hand up in the room'. One boy answered that they would neutralize and another asked 'Are they the same strength?' Susan asked them how they would see if a chemical reaction takes place. She asked one of the girls who replied 'A change of colour'. Susan agreed and then sent one of the boys out of the room on account of something he did which I didn't see. She then asked Paul for another answer. Paul volunteered 'a spark' and another boy gave another answer.

By now the two vapours had met and Susan got pupils to come and look carefully to see 'the white cloud'. One boy asked if the fact that the cloud was nearer one end meant one substance was stronger than the other. Susan replied that this tells us about the speed of travel.

At 2.33 p.m. Susan briefly left the room, returning with the boy she had sent out. She then told the class to get their homework diaries out. For homework they had to draw a labelled diagram, describe the experiment and write a conclusion. To help in this, Susan wrote 'ammonia' and 'concentrated hydrochloric acid' on the board and one boy asked what concentrated meant.

After removing the demonstration to the prep room, Susan got pupils to shut the windows and then spent eight minutes individually giving them their circuit test results – both as marks out of 25 and as National Curriculum levels.

After this she congratulated them as a group on their test results and told them she would go over the test at the beginning of next term to help them with their SATs (see p. 46). A minute later the hooter went and the class was dismissed.

Katie Toland's teaching

This was Katie Toland's first year of teaching. I asked how she was finding Pasmoor School and she replied 'Brilliant, really good. I've thoroughly enjoyed it. Everyone has been really supportive'. Outside of school her main interest, in addition to going away for weekends with friends, was netball which she played at club and county level. When I asked how she liked to teach science she thought carefully and then answered: 'I like to make it practical and I like to make it fun so if it can have some sort of [pause] related it to an everyday incident or if you can put a little story with it . . . not so much the writing. They've got to do that but'

In the classroom Katie exuded enthusiasm and quickly struck up a rapport with pupils. For example, speaking to me about Marc (in one of the Special classes), she said: 'He has a real sense of humour; a superb sense of humour. He again is a real trier but doesn't get the results the girls do. I've seen him in tears . . . calls me "Shortie"!' I asked her 'Do you mind that?' and Katie replied 'He doesn't do it in class . . . when I meet him one to one . . . I got to know him better on the French exchange . . .'

I'd like to describe parts of two of Katie's Year 9 lessons. These have not been chosen at random but were not untypical in terms of the exchanges they revealed between pupils, particularly in respect of two pupils (neither of whom was in the original Year 7 class I studied), whom I shall call Erica and Jason. Jason devoted much of his energies in class to making as many sexually explicit comments as he could. These were said quietly – so as, I presume, to ensure that they wouldn't be overheard by the teacher – and it was only because he sat near the back of the lab that I quite often heard what he was saying.

I could easily have described many excellent lessons of Katie's. However, my focus here is not so much on what Katie was teaching – indeed both these lessons contained a great deal of valid science teaching and most of the pupils worked diligently at their science. Instead, I am interested in how the intellectual opportunities presented and the movement permitted in school science lessons allow pupils to engage in certain conversations and actions with each other.

On 14 November Katie was teaching this class about the elements and the periodic table. She asked them to tell her some properties of metals. Someone said 'hard'. Erica had her hand up. Jason said 'Erica is going to say soft'. Erica, still with her hand up, said to Jason 'I was going to say cold'. Jason giggled and said 'Long and hard and cold' and five seconds later he said, quietly, to Erica 'long and lubricated'. A few minutes later Jason told Erica 'If you want to die, eat 1000 bananas. It's equivalent to one ecstasy tablet'.

Later in the lesson the pupils were given boiling tubes and Jason rubbed his hand up and down the boiling tube and asked 'Erica, what does this remind you of?' Later another boy told Erica 'I'd love to have a worm's eye view of you'. Erica asked him why. 'Because worms are on the ground and could look up your skirt' he replied. Jason then said to this boy 'Worms don't have eyes', which I think was possibly the only valid scientific statement he uttered all lesson, followed by 'Why don't you use a mirror?' At this point Katie called out 'Jason, I can hear your voice over all the others'. A bit later Erica asked one of the boys – the one mentioned on page 52 who was statemented for social reasons – if he had a boyfriend, and later in the lesson she and another boy played at stretching each other's jumpers.

At the end of the lesson Katie told me that Jason was on a contract between the school and his parents (on account of his behaviour) and that he had been arrested the previous week for pulling an airgun on a granny in a shop.

On 27 February Katie Toland had a double period with this class during which they carried out an investigation on factors that affect the rate of respiration in yeast. One of the variables investigated was temperature and when the pupils were planning their investigation I heard Jason say 'Let's put some ice on her [Erica's] tit'. Later in the lesson Jason tried to persuade Erica to put some ice on her nipples to get them to stand erect. Later, another boy, with Erica's consent, fingered her necklace in front of her neck. Katie spotted him and told him to get on with his work.

Later in the same lesson, some of the boys started trying (with some success) to put ice-cubes down the fronts of some of the girls' blouses or down their necks. Some of the girls retaliated in like vein. Jason tried to engage Erica in a conversation about her bikini. He succeeded in putting an ice-cube in the breast pocket of Erica's shirt. She removed it and said 'I don't want any more ice, thank you'. I think she wanted Katie Toland to overhear this, but Katie didn't. Erica then wandered around the room, ice-cube in hand, looking for an opportunity to put it down Jason's neck. Katie spotted her and ticked her off. Later in the same lesson one of the boys called the teacher 'Mum' by mistake. He was embarrassed and got teased by Jason, whom he eventually slapped.

Pupils' exercise books

Paul's exercise books contained a range of comments such as 'A good effort', 'A clear diagram. Well done', 'Take care with spelling & presentation', 'Draw in pencil please' and 'Good'. His write-up of the ammonia and hydrochloric demonstration described above is shown in Figure 4.4.

Richard clearly took a lot of care over his written work and his exercise books were filled with comments such as 'Great!', 'Excellent', 'You have some excellent work, keep it up Richard. Please collect a Merit from me', 'A good explanation' and 'Accurate work. You show a good level of understanding'. One of his exercise books contained abusive comments clearly written in by

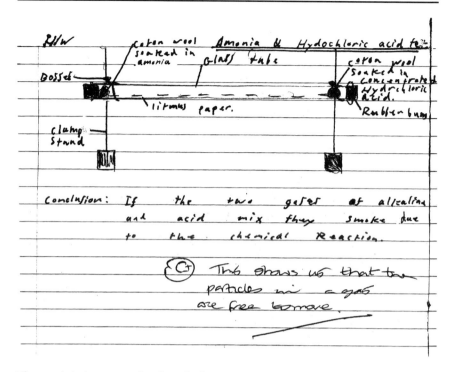

Figure 4.4 An example of Paul's homework

another pupil. His cover pages for each new topic were a delight and one of them is shown in Figure 4.5.

Sue occasionally had work missing but her exercise books mostly recorded a series of 'Good's. An example of her work is provided in Figure 4.6.

Susan de Von's and Katie Toland's Special class

The Special class that Susan de Von and Katie Toland taught had 25 pupils, 11 of them girls and 14 of them boys. Five of the pupils I was especially interested in were in it: Burt, Catherine, Marc, Nicky and Robert.

Pupils' exercise books

There was a consistent theme to the comments on Burt's pieces of work in his exercise book: 'A good effort, although please make sure that you always include information from the question in your answers. Take care with spelling', 'You show a good understanding, but you must ensure that you answer in full sentences' and 'Good answers, it is a pity the work is not

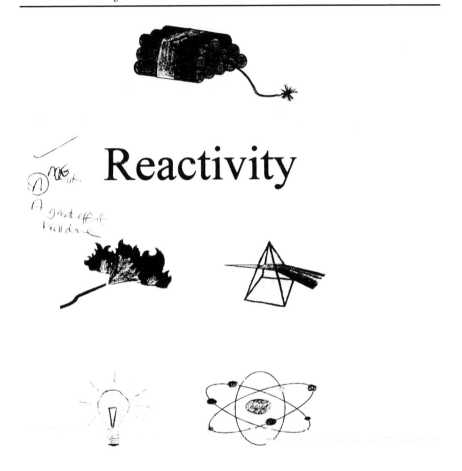

Figure 4.5 Richard always took a great deal of care over any piece of work

complete'. Considering Burt's spelling on the human reproduction test in Year 7 (see p. 30), I was impressed and encouraged at how much this had improved. A sample of his writing is given in Figure 4.7.

Catherine's work was carefully written up and received a series of positive comments: 'Good', 'V. detailed descriptions of these expts [experiments]', 'Thorough & clear answers', 'These diagrams could do with being tidied up a little' and 'A very good set of answers. You have understood the work well'. An example of her work is given in Figure 4.8.

The work in Marc's exercise books received a number of positive comments though there were indications that sometimes work had not been completed or fully understood: 'Good. A', 'What does this show?', 'Good A', 'O.K. but no information about sedimentary rocks. B−', 'What about the magnesium? Describe this expt.', 'You should also have completed description etc of

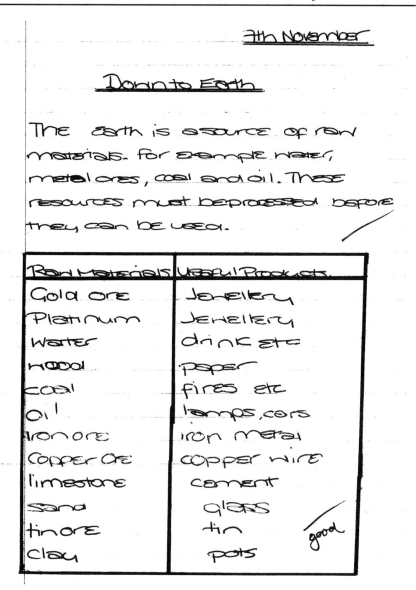

Figure 4.6 A typical piece of Sue's work

Thermite Reaction. Please do so.' and 'A Accurate word equations'. An example of his work is provided in Figure 4.9.

Nicky's exercise books revealed a string of positive comments: 'Good work Nicky. Well done', 'Great!', 'Good A', 'B+ A clear account. You show a very

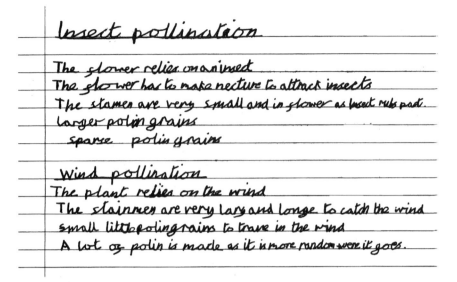

Insect pollination

The flower relies on an insect
The flower has to make necture to attrack insects
The stamen are very small and in flower as insect rubs past.
Larger polin grains
    sparce   polin grains

Wind pollination
The plant relies on the wind
The stainmen are very large and longe to catch the wind
small little polin grains to trave in the wind
A lot of polin is made as it is more random were it goes.

Figure 4.7   A typical piece of Burt's Year 9 writing. Compare with his spelling on the Year 7 human reproduction test (see p. 30)

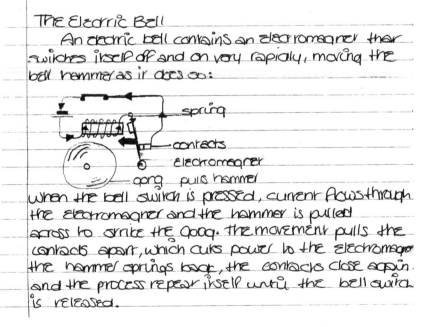

The Electric Bell
    An electric bell contains an electromagnet that switches itself off and on very rapidly, moving the bell hammer as it does so:

spring

contacts

electromagnet

gong   pulls hammer

When the bell switch is pressed, current flows through the electromagnet and the hammer is pulled across to strike the gong. The movement pulls the contacts apart, which cuts power to the electromagnet the hammer springs back, the contacts close again, and the process repeat itself until the bell switch is released.

Figure 4.8   A typical example of Catherine's work

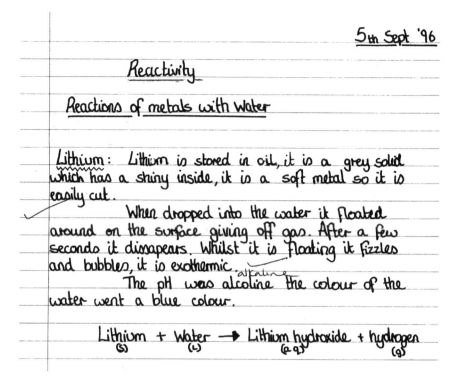

5th Sept '96

Reactivity

Reactions of metals with water

Lithium: Lithium is stored in oil, it is a grey solid which has a shiny inside, it is a soft metal so it is easily cut.
When dropped into the water it floated around on the surface giving off gas. After a few seconds it dissapears. Whilst it is floating it fizzles and bubbles, it is exothermic.
The pH was alcaline the colour of the water went a blue colour.

Lithium + Water → Lithium hydroxide + hydrogen
(s)   (L)   (aq)   (g)

Figure 4.9 A piece of Marc's work from the very beginning of Year 9

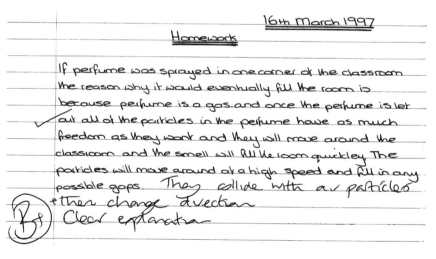

16th March 1997

Homework

If perfume was sprayed in one corner of the classroom the reason why it would eventually fill the room is because perfume is a gas. and once the perfume is let out all of the particles in the perfume have as much freedom as they want and they will move around the classroom and the smell will fill the room quickley. The particles will move around at a high speed and fill in any possible gaps. They collide with av particles & then change direction
Clear explanation

Figure 4.10 An example of Nicky's homework. The quality of the work is typical for her but the length is shorter than usual

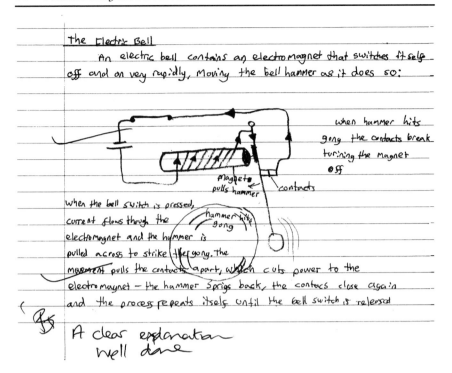

The Electric Bell

An electric bell contains an electromagnet that switches itself off and on very rapidly, moving the bell hammer as it does so:

when hammer hits gong the contacts break turning the magnet off

Magnet pulls hammer   contacts

when the bell switch is pressed, current flows through the electromagnet and the hammer is pulled across to strike the gong. The movement pulls the contacts apart, which cuts power to the electromagnet – the hammer springs back, the contacts close again and the process repeats itself until the bell switch is released

A clear explanation well done

Figure 4.11 An example of Robert's work from the second half of Year 9 by which time his work had improved considerably compared with earlier in the year

good level of understanding' and 'A Excellent understanding. Well done'. An example of a homework of hers is given in Figure 4.10.

At the beginning of the year Robert's work attracted a number of very critical comments: 'C – What about magnesium? You should have written a conclusion leading to an <u>order</u> or reactivity', 'Use <u>pencil</u> when drawing tables <u>please</u>', 'C Please see me Robert – this work is not of the standard that I would expect from somebody in a Special Set' and 'You really must be prepared to put more detail & effort into your written answers'. As the year went on, though, the comments improved: ' B+ A good pair of solutions. Please use a ruler for diagrams' and 'Clear diagrams. Well done'. Figure 4.11 shows a piece of Robert's work from the second half of the year.

Roland Newman's and James Western's Special class

The Special class that Roland Newman and James Western taught had 27 pupils, 14 of them girls and 13 of them boys. Five of the pupils I was especially

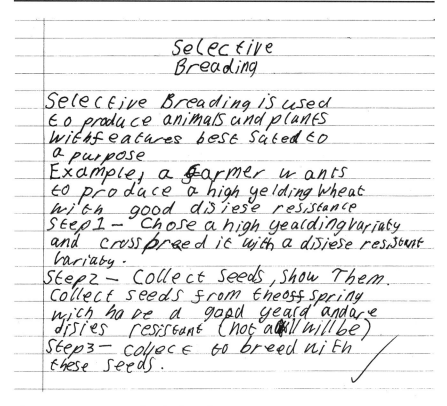

Figure 4.12 An example of Edward's work showing a good level of scientific understanding along with below average spelling

interested in were in it: Edward, Ian, Jack, Mary and Rebecca. Mary had therefore been moved up a set from Year 8.

Pupils' exercise books

Edward's exercise books contained a range of teacher comments: 'C Good attempt', 'B – Reasonable explanation. Learn spelling of PARTICLE', 'Pencil diagrams Edward' and 'Good detail, and I like the inclusion of the specimens. What other methods are used?' Figure 4.12 shows a representative example of Edward's writing.

Ian's work received a somewhat mixed set of responses: 'A An interesting collection of plants Ian', 'C+ Does this have a stigma? How will pollen get to the ovary?', 'Full sentences please' and 'Good attempt, but you could tie the evidence to the theory more closely'. An example of his work is shown in Figure 4.13.

Jack's work also received a range of responses. Typical comments were 'B+

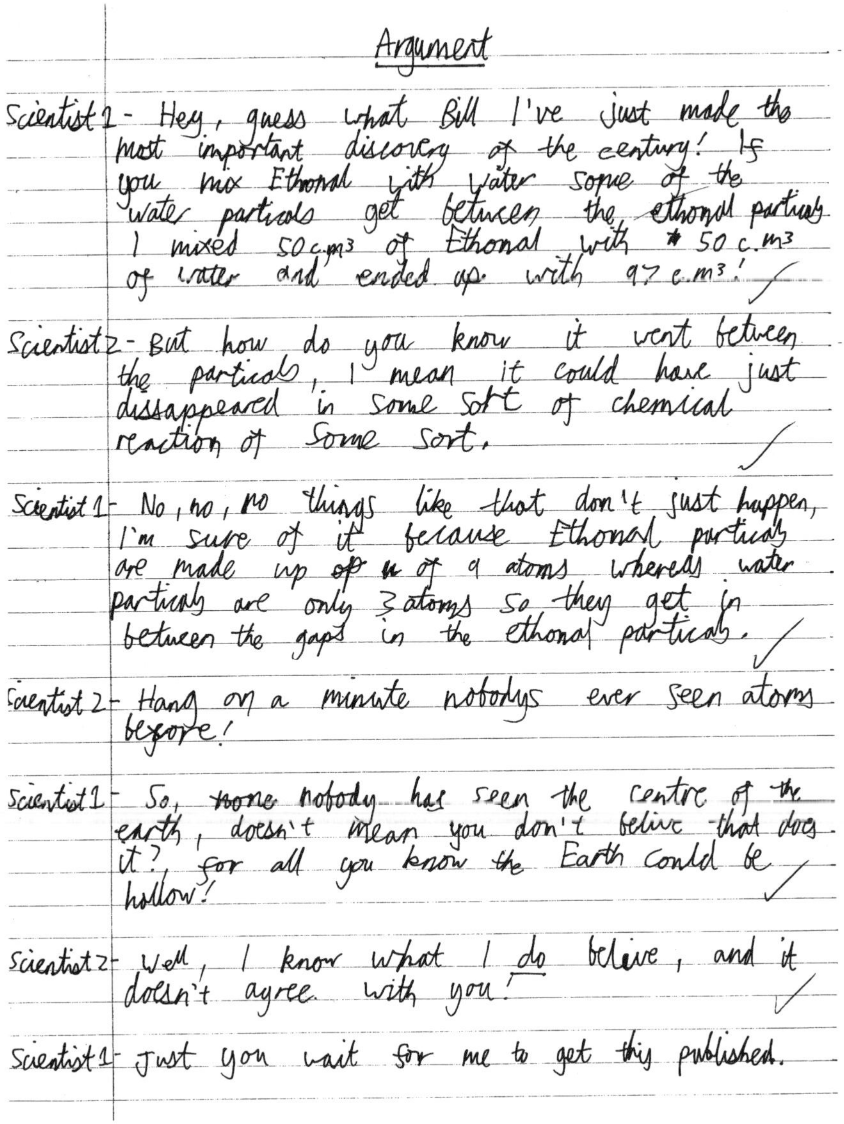

<u>Argument</u>

Scientist 1 - Hey, guess what Bill I've just made the most important discovery of the century! If you mix Ethonal with water some of the water particals get between the ethonal particals I mixed 50 c.m3 of Ethonal with ⚹ 50 c.m3 of water and ended up with 97 c.m3!

Scientist 2 - But how do you know it went between the particals, I mean it could have just dissappeared in some sort of chemical reaction of some sort.

Scientist 1 - No, no, no things like that don't just happen, I'm sure of it because Ethonal particals are made up of ⚹ of 9 atoms whereas water particals are only 3 atoms so they get in between the gaps in the ethonal particals.

Scientist 2 - Hang on a minute nobodys ever seen atoms before!

Scientist 1 - So, ~~none~~ nobody has seen the centre of the earth, doesn't mean you don't belive that does it?, for all you know the Earth could be hollow!

Scientist 2 - Well, I know what I do belive, and it doesn't agree with you!

Scientist 1 - Just you wait for me to get this published.

Figure 4.13 A nice piece of scientific writing by Ian

A good idea Jack, clearly explained', 'C Jack, when you describe a pattern try to explain it', 'Needs a little more detail. C', 'A Well explained' and 'B Good explanation. You were asked to do a diagram showing particles'. An example of his work is given in Figure 4.14.

Mary evidently took a lot of care over how her work was presented and received lots of positive feedback: 'Good diagrams', 'A+ An excellent

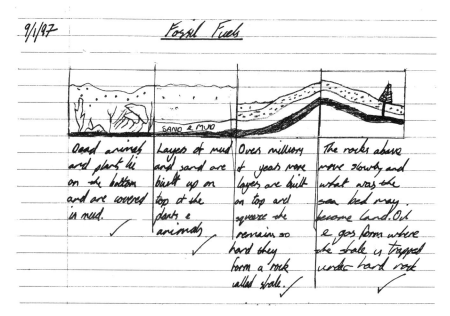

9/1/97   *Fossil Fuels*

SAND & MUD

| Dead animals and plants lie on the bottom and are covered in mud. ✓ | Layers of mud and sand are built up on top of the plants e animals ✓ | Over millions of years more layers are built on top and squeeze the remains so hard they form a rock called shale. ✓ | The rocks above move slowly and what was the sea bed may become land. Oil e gas form where the shale is trapped under hard rock ✓ |

Figure 4.14 An example of Jack's work

homework. Well thought out and presented', 'Good classwork', 'Good' and 'Excellent detail on rock features'. An example of a homework of hers at the beginning of Year 9, which also affords a description of her home, is provided in Figure 4.15.

Rebecca's work received positive comments: 'Well developed Theory A', 'Good clear drawings' and 'B Good explanation', for example. A portion of her writing, taken from an extended piece on 'Balanced forces', is given in Figure 4.16.

Comments on Year 9 science lessons

Pupils as sexual beings

I would like to emphasize that sexually explicit comments were heard in many lessons, *not* just those taught by Katie Toland. The sexually explicit comments I heard were, almost without exception, made by the boys. For example, in the lesson taught by James Western on 24 January, one of the boys had spilled Tipp-Ex on a table and was clearing it up. Another boy called out 'There's a white, creamy, mess on the table' and there was lots of laughter from some of the boys. Later in the same lesson, when looking at the making of iron in the context of displacement reactions (i.e. getting iron from iron ore), one of the boys called out 'Slag. It says slag here' (slag is the waste

Homework   8ᵗʰ September 96

A Tour of the Plants in My House.

My House is about 300 years old and was two workmens cottages until they were joined together to become one house (so we have two sets of stairs) All the beams and upstairs floor are made of old ships timber which still have some bolts left in them.

In the kitchen we have a couple of venus fly traps to keep off any flys off the food and hanging off the ceiling we have an assortment of dried herbs and scottish thumb we also have a large vase of white roses in one window.   which plant grows?

In the hall way we have a small bush like plant. which has no name tag so I don't know what its called. Moving on past the bath room (which has a pot of FAke flowers in it) to the study.

Now the study only has a big vase of 3 year old dried flowers which are so battered about I can't tell what they are! in the study something has a smaller vase of some purple flowers or imon luives.

In the lounge we have another large vase of roses, except these ones are pink. Then up past the play room, showerroom, my sisters room, At and into my brothers room which has a small green plant with yellow flowers   . and its surrounded by ivy. Come down past my room and back threw the kitchen, to the door. If you come outside you will see the roof is made of straw.

Figure 4.15 An autobiographical piece from Mary

product in this reaction). There was laughter from the boys on his table and one of them called out 'What's a slag, Mr Western?' James quietened them down and explained to the whole class, absolutely straight-faced, what slag, in the scientific sense, is.

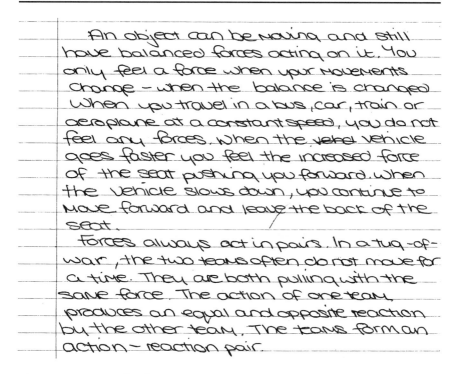

An object can be moving and still have balanced forces acting on it. You only feel a force when your movements change – when the balance is changed. When you travel in a bus, car, train or aeroplane at a constant speed, you do not feel any forces. When the vehicle goes faster you feel the increased force of the seat pushing you forward. When the vehicle slows down, you continue to move forward and leave the back of the seat.

Forces always act in pairs. In a tug-of-war, the two teams often do not move for a time. They are both pulling with the same force. The action of one team produces an equal and opposite reaction by the other team. The teams form an action – reaction pair.

Figure 4.16 Part of Rebecca's two pages of A4 on 'Balanced forces'

The message I understood James Western to be giving was that such use of language was not acceptable and he was not going to join in joking about it. At the same time, pupils were not punished for using such language. Perhaps the implicit lesson both boys and girls were learning was not that certain language is absolutely unacceptable but that it is inappropriate in certain contexts, such as school science lessons.

That 13- to 14-year-olds are sexual beings is hardly surprising news to anyone who knows much about them. Indeed there have been careful studies both in the UK (Herbert 1989) and in the USA (Astor *et al.* 1999) documenting sexual harassment and sexual violence towards schoolgirls. Nevertheless, I admit that I was surprised at the sustained and extended nature of the abuse in some of the science lessons I was observing. In part my surprise was because it has been found, as common sense would suggest, that the areas in a school where violence and sexual harassment are most likely to take place are where adults are not present – hallways, parking lots, playgrounds and school buses – rather than classrooms during lessons (Astor *et al.* 1999).

But then I found myself thinking: was I right simply to identify the incidences described above as sexual harassment or abuse by boys of girls? While a high proportion of boys (perhaps around 20–35 per cent) made sexually suggestive remarks, they were still in a minority. Indeed, most examples of sexual 'banter' were performed by boys not for the 'benefit' of girls but with boys as the audience. As other researchers have noted, sexist jokes between boys serve to augment male bonding (Kehily and Nayak 1997). And it was only a very few individuals who behaved as Jason did, so far as I could tell.

In any event, was I oversimplifying when I saw Jason's behaviour as sexual harassment? I don't think so and yet it would be wrong for me to portray Erica as a passive victim of male sexual aggression. Although her attempt to put ice down Jason's back may not have been successful, she was more than capable herself of initiating what some would describe as mildly flirtatious behaviour (e.g. stretching a boy's jumper as described above) and of asking questions about boyfriends to, I think, embarrass a boy – again as described above. The way I came to see such behaviours was that both boys and girls used the space within classrooms to define themselves and their relationships with others. As a generalization, boys had more space than girls but there were many exceptions.

The impressions made by girls and boys on their science teachers

On page 25 I showed how the Year 7 boys made more of an impression on Stephen Benton than did the girls. I was interested to see whether this was the case for other teachers too.

By the end of Year 9 I had carried out a total of 19 interviews with teachers, student teachers and learning support assistants. Fifteen people participated in these interviews as three teachers and one learning support assistant were interviewed twice. I went through each interview, taking into account the relative number of girls and boys in the relevant classes, and made a judgement as to whether girls or boys had made more of an impression. I took into account both the number of comments made and their detail. One interview was not analysed here because it was with Roland Newman before he had taught any of the classes I was observing. My judgement as to whether boys or girls made more of an impact on the teachers or not is given in Table 4.1.

From Table 4.1 I conclude the following:

- For none of the teachers, learning support assistants or student teachers did girls make more of an impact than boys.
- For 8 of the 15 teachers, learning support assistants and student teachers boys made more of an impact than girls.
- There is some evidence that female teachers were less likely than male teachers to allow boys to make more of an impact on them than girls.

My judgement was that the reason that boys on average made more of an impression on their teachers than did girls, and so were more likely to be talked about when I asked teachers to describe pupils in their classes, was simply because boys were more likely to misbehave, to call out answers to a teacher's questions, to fail to do their homework and generally to attract

Table 4.1   Analysis as to whether girls or boys make more of an impact on their teachers

Teacher	Characteristics	Did girls or boys make more of an impact?
Helen Coombs	f, et, 1	Even
Susan de Von	f, et, 1	Even
Hannah Thomson	f, et, 1	Boys (slightly)
Katie Toland	f, it, 1	Even
Stephen Benton	m, et, 2	Boys (strongly)
Roland Newman	m, et, 1	Boys (slightly)
James Western	m, et, 2	Boys (slightly)
Bernadette McLaughlin	f, el, 1	Boys (strongly)
Lakisha Mistry	f, el, 2	Even
Mandy Bickenstaff	f, s, 1	Boys (slightly)
Lucie Moore	f, s, 1	Even
Di Peters	f, s, 1	Even
Tessa Ratcliffe	f, s, 1	Even
Vicky Woods	f, s, 1	Boys (slightly)
Mark Sindall	m, s, 1	Boys (strongly)

Note: f = female; m = male; et = experienced teacher; it = inexperienced teacher (first year); el = experienced learning support assistant; s = student teacher; 1 = interviewed once; 2 = interviewed twice.

attention to themselves. Of course, there were many exceptions to this. Of the pupils I was following, Burt, Ian, Paul, Richard and Robert could be said to be quite 'quiet' in class. But then so could just about all the girls I was following. As a result, teachers ended up paying more attention to such pupils as George, Peter and Rodney.

SATs

To a large extent as the year went on, Year 9 science lessons at Pasmoor School became increasingly dominated by SATs – the national assessments in English, mathematics and science carried out towards the end of Year 9. The science SATs were on 12 May and consisted of two papers, one of 60 minutes sat in the morning and one of 60 minutes sat in the afternoon. These papers were available at two tiers of difficulty so that each pupil either sat two papers, each of which was designed to discriminate between Levels 3–6, or two designed to discriminate between Levels 5–7. Pupils were given an eight-page A5 booklet by the science department listing topics to revise and providing 'revision hints'. In addition, pupils were encouraged to buy one of two 96-page revision booklets through the science department before the Easter 'holidays' (Joyner 1995, 1996).

I found myself having rather mixed views about the Year 9 SATs. On the one hand, a tremendous amount of effort goes into their production and there is little doubt that as assessment instruments they are more reliable than any tests an individual school could come up with. A national, independent evaluation of the 1995 and 1996 science SATs found that they 'generally operated very satisfactorily both in terms of the general requirements for such tests (validity in relation to the national curriculum, absence of bias, linguistic demands, quality of mark schemes etc.) and in terms of the operation of individual questions' (Radnor *et al.* 1996: 92).

However, there are three main problems with the Year 9 science SATs. The first derives from the form of assessment used. To ensure that the marking is reliable (in the sense that independent markers would be almost certain to award the same number of marks) each question carries only a small number of marks. As a result, the questions are rather 'narrow' in the sense that credit is almost never given for imaginative or creative thinking or for linking ideas from different areas of science. Indeed, the questions almost never give room for such originality or relating of ideas. That the tests should be limited in this way was not the original intention of those who devised the framework for National Curriculum assessment. However, a complicated series of events led to political pressure in the 1990s for the tests to be short, easy to administer and quick to mark (Black 1995). Thus they became and thus they remain to this day.

A second problem with the science SATs, whether at Year 2, Year 6 or Year 9 is that they mostly present a 'pure' vision of science, a science largely divorced from technology and the everyday concerns of people. A science that instead occupies itself with the passage of light through prisms (refraction), Janet-and-John-like gardens (food chains) and the endless excitement of droplets of water condensing on cold glass (changing materials).

As someone who sat for several years on the vetting panel that helped set the Year 6 science SATs, I acknowledge the difficulties of trying to devise more meaningful questions. Any attempt to introduce a note of reality into a question almost invariably led to howls of protest either along the lines of 'Teachers won't be expecting that' or on the theme of 'We can't produce an unambiguous answer for that'.

In such circumstances, question setters and schools become locked in a framework from which attempts to escape to the rest of the known universe are unlikely to succeed (Reiss 2000). This framework is reinforced by annual reports from the Qualifications and Curriculum Authority thoughtfully telling teachers how to help next year's pupils to score better (e.g. Qualifications and Curriculum Authority 1998).

The third problem with the Year 9 science SATs is that most schools, and Pasmoor School was no exception, devote a lot of classroom time to getting pupils to revise for them. The same large-scale national evaluation of the 1996 Year 9 SATs (Radnor *et al.* 1996: 138) found that:

Table 4.2 Questions asked by me of the Year 9 parents

1(a) How do you think [your child] has got on this last year at Pasmoor School?
1(b) [As 1a but specifically in science.]
2 What are your opinions of Pasmoor School?
3 What would you like [your child's] science lessons at Pasmoor School to consist of?
4 What are your hopes for [your child] for the future?
5 What do you see are the main functions of schools?

- 98 per cent of teachers had practice sessions, using past or sample papers;
- 88 per cent of teachers spent time explaining the timing, rubric and structure of the test;
- 84 per cent of teachers prepared pupils for examination conditions;
- 73 per cent of teachers built into their lesson planning the sort of language used in the tests.

It can be argued that such practices have their uses. They make it more likely that pupils will learn what they have been taught and they prepare them for the joys awaiting them at GCSE. Certainly, had I been teaching I would have done all of this, as the teachers at Pasmoor School did.

What would parents like science lessons to consist of?

There has been a tremendous amount of debate both in the UK and worldwide in recent years about what should be contained in school science curricula (Black and Atkin 1996; Millar and Osborne 1998). However, parental and pupil views about what should be in the Science curriculum seem rarely if ever to be listened to, let alone taken account of. Accordingly, one of the questions I asked parents in the end of the Year 9 interview was 'What would you like [your child]'s science lessons at Pasmoor School to consist of?' (see Table 4.2).

The responses I got can (with a certain difficulty!) be classified into six categories, as follows. Five of the parents (Burt's mother, Jack's father, Marc's mother, Richard's mother, Sue's mother) gave responses with elements that I have put into two separate categories.

Relevant to life

I suppose things that are relevant like the pollution; things that are going to affect their future. If they're made aware of what's happening. So really a relevant content for their life, really.

(Catherine's mother)

I think at this age it needs to have a relevance . . . they need to see its relevance . . . I gave up science because I couldn't see any relevance and I wasn't encouraged to.

(Marc's mother)

I know. How science impacts on their daily life.

(Marc's stepfather)

What about practical things like showing children how to wire up plugs, how their CD player works?

(Nicky's mother)

Like power generation . . . how does electricity get made.

(Nicky's father)

Ooh. My goodness. I suppose I'd like something relevant for what she ends up doing . . . when I did science I thought 'Why am I doing this?' because I knew I wasn't going to be a scientist . . . we were forced to do it.

(Rebecca's mother)

Environmental matters . . . perhaps matters related to health.

(Richard's mother)

Medical . . . when you think of diseases like cancer.

(Sue's mother)

Unsure

God. I wouldn't know!

(Edward's mother)

That's a jolly good question. I'm not scientific.

(George's mother)

I've no idea . . . I dunno; everything.

(Jack's mother)

Gosh. Having given up science at the end of the third year . . .

(Marc's mother)

What sort of question is that?! . . . I don't know . . . I'm a country boy.

(Martin's father)

Blimey!

(Mary's stepfather)

I don't know what they do.

(Paul's mother)

Some practical work

Balance between the [content] and experiments.

(Burt's mother)

Balance between doing experiments and allowing them [pupils] the freedom to discuss.

(Jack's father)

You just hope they do some practical work. I think he'd like experiments rather than learning from textbooks.

(Robert's father)

I'd like them to be related to projects . . . it should be related to design, practically related to design . . . theory later.

(Rodney's mother)

For future scientists

As to the subject matter, it could be vast . . . People from university wanting the A level people to provide certain things and A level people wanting the schools to [provide a base for A levels].

(Burt's mother)

More keeping his enthusiasm going so he doesn't come back saying 'I've learned a pile of facts' . . . so you end up with more creative scientists at the end of the day . . . enthusiasm's not enough. You have to have academic knowledge and ability as well.

(Ian's mother)

Engineering for those going into engineering . . . biology for those going into medicine.

(Richard's mother)

Academic science

I think understanding scientific principles through recognized examples.

(Edward's father)

The key thing you want is that you can explain observations you make on a large scale by making observations at a small level, for example in chemistry . . . link through to how you create models.

(Jack's father)

Interest

Umm. Well, I always think about space . . . that intrigues me.

(Sue's mother)

Comment on what parents would like science lessons to consist of

Of the six categories, the largest was 'Relevant to life'. Encouragingly, in my view, this is also the consensus among science educators. Many of the science teachers at Pasmoor School made significantly more links between what they were teaching and the world outside of school than is often the case in school science (see Mayoh and Knutton 1997). Among science educators it is generally agreed that the prime function of a school science curriculum when it is mandatory for all pupils – i.e. at present up to the age of 16 in England and Wales – is to provide a science education that is relevant for all pupils both now and once they become adults. Such a curriculum would look rather different from the one we have at present! This is a point I will return to in subsequent chapters. At present we have a science curriculum for 5–16-year-olds that does its best both to be relevant to life and to cater for the minority of school pupils who will go on to become scientists.

A substantial number of parents were unsure what they would like school science lessons to consist of. Perhaps unsurprisingly, such responses were especially common from parents like George's mother, Marc's mother and Mary's stepfather, who had given up science at school at the earliest opportunity or who, like Jack's mother, had received a particularly impoverished school science education (see parental biographies on pp. 57–64). Interestingly, only two replies suggested that school science should be about academic science. One of these came from a male research geophysicist (Jack's father) and the other from a male who runs his own computer company (Edward's father).

Key points

- There was a large amount of excellent science teaching in Year 9, as in all other years.
- Analysis of pupils' textbooks showed a wide range of pupil industry and attainment.
- Some female pupils received a stream of sexually explicit comments and suggestions from certain boys.
- Boys tended to make more of an impression on their teachers across Years 7 to 9 than did girls, and this was especially likely to be the case when the teacher was male. However, this was only the case for some boys and for some teachers.
- As Year 9 wore on, the science SATs had an increasingly strong influence on what went on in the classroom.
- Many parents were unsure as to what sort of science they would like their children to be taught but the most popular criterion was that it should be relevant to life.

5

Year 10: 'First, I have to cover the syllabus'

It was pointed out that there is a possibility that children could
answer the questions through personal experiences and therefore
not using scientific understanding.
(School Curriculum and Assessment Authority 1995: Note 3.9)

The background to Year 10

Year 10 marked the formal start of the two years of GCSE though the science
department at Pasmoor School had, in fact, made a start on the GCSE science
syllabus in the time remaining at the end of Year 9 after the science SAT on
12 May.

At the start of Year 10, the 17 remaining pupils from the original 21 I had
started with in Year 7 were spread over six classes. Most state schools in England enter their pupils for Double Award GCSE science and Pasmoor School
was no exception. Of the 17 pupils 15 were doing Double Award GCSE science, which meant that each pupil would end up with two GCSEs of the same
grade for science – e.g. DD or BB.

The remaining two pupils, Ian and Paul, were instead doing Triple Award
science, for reasons explained below. This meant that they would end up with
three GCSEs, one in biology, one in chemistry and one in physics. These three
subjects were assessed independently so it was perfectly possible to get different grades in them. Some of Ian and Paul's science lessons were in the normal
Double Award classes and some in extra Triple Award classes.

Irrespective of whether they were doing Double Award or Triple Award science, all pupils had three teachers, one for biology, one for chemistry and one
for physics. The pattern I shall follow in this chapter is, as in Chapters 3 and 4
to look at these classes in approximate order of ability/attainment. I say
'approximate' because although some movements of pupils were made by
teachers between classes during the year, each class contained quite a range
of abilities.

As in Chapters 3 and 4, I shall describe an example of a lesson of each of the four teachers whose science lessons I saw for the first time during the year in question, i.e. during Year 10, in this chapter. Each of these four examples is drawn randomly from my notes. But my focus in this chapter is largely on the 17 pupils I was now following for the fourth year: on how their teachers saw them and on how they themselves felt about their science lessons.

The one teacher described in Chapter 4 who had left by the start of Year 10 was James Western. The circumstances of his leaving were extremely painful to him and I spent some time talking with him after his departure and ended up writing job references for him.

Rumours were rife among pupils as to why James had left and I wondered whether to spend some time here describing his side of the story. In the end, I decided not to. In large part this was because I hadn't discussed with the headteacher at Pasmoor School her reasons for wanting him to leave and so I decided it wouldn't be fair to provide only James' version of events. The reason I didn't ask the headteacher for her understanding of events was because I was worried that if I did that she might withdraw permission for me to continue my study. I dare say this was entirely paranoid on my part but I decided to play safe and avoid raising the question of James' departure. Nor did any member of the science department ever talk to me about why he had left.

Peter and Rodney's class

Peter and Rodney were taught in a class that at the beginning of the year had 12 pupils, three of whom were girls and nine of whom were boys. The class included George and Martin. However, both George and Martin were moved up a set during the year and so left this class. Peter and Rodney's teachers were Roland Newman for biology, Fiona Roberts for chemistry and Christine Evans for physics.

Fiona Roberts' teaching

Fiona Roberts had originally come to Pasmoor School in January 1989 as deputy head of science. She then had a baby and left, subsequently returning part-time with a series of one-year contracts. I asked her if that felt OK with her and she said that it did. 'I wouldn't struggle to get a job [i.e. she would be able to get one easily] if I left here'.

I found that easy to believe. Fiona communicated chemistry extremely clearly and was very alert to what was going on in her lessons, as a result of which she got even Peter and Rodney to pay attention and behave. When I asked her what she was trying to achieve in science lessons she replied:

> Ooh. Now that's an interesting question. First, I have to cover the syllabus. So there's content but there's also skills. Not just science skills.

With a group like Rodney's there's also social skills . . . not just for Rodney but with others in that group [you serve as a] role model . . . So you've got the education for exams, but you've also got the educating for life. They're all lovely kids. I don't want them to . . . for example, get the sack for silly things they should have got out of their system at school . . . interested, relevance. Inspired is a bit strong but enthusiastic about the subject matter. I might have a bit of difficulty with that group but! And I want them to fulfil their potential whatever that potential is.

A typical example of one of Fiona's lessons was the single lesson I observed on 5 December from 1.10 p.m. to 2.00 p.m. At this stage both George and Martin were still in this class. However, Peter was absent so there were just 11 pupils present that day.

At the beginning of the lesson, Fiona gathered the class round the front and explained that this afternoon they were going to look at the question of 'How does the temperature of a solvent affect how much solute it can dissolve?' She explained that the solvent (a new word she introduced to them) would be water and the solute would be salt. She asked Martin to make a prediction. He replied 'The higher temperature will go up'. Fiona asked someone else and one of the girls quietly put her hands round Rodney's waist and then let go.

Fiona explained that a prediction would be something like 'The higher the temperature the more salt will dissolve'. She then asked them how they would know that no more salt could dissolve. One boy offered to answer and said by looking at the thermometer. Fiona said no. One girl said by looking to see if there's a pile of salt and Fiona agreed.

At 1.27 p.m. the pupils started their practical work. George and Rodney worked together and Martin worked with one of the other boys. Fiona had already written on the board a heading, a diagram of the experimental set-up, the method, a results table for pupils to fill in and the labelled axes of a graph for them to complete. The results table told them to carry out the experiment at six temperatures, namely 30°C, 45°C, 55°C, 70°C, 85°C and 95°C, and each of the six groups carried out the practical at one temperature. One boy worked on his own; all other pupils worked in pairs.

During the practical, for which Fiona insisted the pupils wore safety goggles, she circulated among the groups. At one point Rodney asked if he could write up the method in his own words and Fiona replied that she'd prefer it if he wrote what she had written on the board which was:

150ml of water was heated to different temperatures, the heat was removed and we saw how many spatulas of salt would dissolve as we stirred. We stopped when no more would dissolve.

Watching the groups, it was clear to me that two of them – the boy working on his own and a pair of boys – had added too much salt. One of the boys in the pair spent quite a while desperately stirring the mixture in an attempt to persuade more salt to dissolve.

By 1.52 p.m. most groups had finished their practical work and were tidying away their apparatus while Fiona collated their results on the board as follows:

30°C = 78;   45°C = 70;   55°C = 72
70°C =   85°C = 85;   95°C = 98

At 1.56 p.m. Fiona gathered the pupils round the front. She pointed out that one result was missing (I think this was the pair who had added far too much salt) and said that one seemed not to be what was expected (this was the boy working on his own). She then asked them what they would expect the 70°C to be. The class agreed a figure of 77 and Fiona wrote '(77) estimate' as the entry. She then explained that it was not surprising that their results weren't exactly as expected, saying that, for instance, the groups had different understandings as to what was meant by a spatula-full.

At 1.59 p.m. Fiona got the pupils to write down that their homework was to finish writing up the experiment including doing a graph and a conclusion. At 2.00 p.m. the hooter sounded and at 2.01 p.m. the pupils started to leave.

Christine Evans' teaching

Christine Evans only arrived at Pasmoor School in October 1997, being the successor to James Western. This was her first teaching job and when I interviewed her at the end of the year she, not surprisingly, described herself as 'shattered' but went on to add that she was enjoying it and appreciating having 'lots of other teachers to ask ideas of'.

Christine described herself as a 'people person' and said that outside of school she played the cello, played in an orchestra, sang Gilbert and Sullivan and did a whole variety of dancing – ballroom, tap and rock 'n' roll.

In science lessons she said she was trying to get pupils 'understanding the subject, getting on their wavelength, helping them to enjoy it though they don't seem to sometimes. When you're starting out, that's enough!'

A typical example of one of Christine's lessons was that of 17 June from 9.35 to 10.25 a.m. with which she introduced the new topic of 'Electricity'. By now not only had George and Martin moved up a set but Peter had left on account of moving to another school. Another boy had joined the set and one of the girls only arrived at 10.20 a.m. (having been at a careers interview), so for most of the lesson there were just nine pupils, seven of whom were boys.

After quietening down the group and taking the register, Christine told them that if they didn't behave well they would lose some of their break. She then wrote 'Electricity' on the blackboard and told them to 'brainstorm' by writing everything they knew about electricity for a minute. She then collated their thoughts, *en route* twice confiscating things from pupils and making threats about missing their break.

Christine then told them that she had done some magic – 'abracadabra' – and blown up some charges millions of times. At this point she produced some approximately 5cm circular cardboard discs: blue ones with a − written on them and orange ones with a + written on them. She explained that actually a charge is a tiny, tiny particle.

At various times during the lesson, whenever a certain amount of misbehaviour had taken place, Christine added on another half minute to a record of how long the class would be kept in for. At one point one of the boys complained that it wasn't fair that they would all be kept in.

After getting the pupils to copy a couple of paragraphs she had written on the board about static electricity, Christine then got one of the boys to volunteer to come forward. She told him that she would stick things all over him, but nowhere 'embarrassing'. She then stuck two of the cardboard negative charges on him and two of the cardboard positive charges on him. She explained how if he rubbed his shoe on the carpet the negative charges would pass to the carpet. Christine got the pupils to appreciate that, as a result, the boy would be positively charged and the carpet negatively charged. She then showed how if his hand touched a metal rod with negative charges on it, these negative charges would move into his hand and give him a shock.

Christine asked for another volunteer and Rodney stepped forward, one of the two girls complaining that this was 'sexist'. Christine then got Rodney to act at driving a car and, by question and answer, got the pupils to think how he could get a shock. The girl who complained at not being given a role – a girl who had been described to me by a Year 9 female teacher as 'A tart! . . . very showy and attention seeking' – was then allowed by Christine to come and sit next to Rodney.

This girl was then given the job of sticking positive and negative charges onto Rodney. She put two on his head, one onto each hand and the last two on his feet. By question and answer, Christine got the class to see that as the car moves along, the negative charges are left on the road. Finally, to end the role-play, Christine got Rodney to leave the car and he did a fine impression of someone getting a lethal electric shock.

Christine then gave the pupils eight minutes to draw three examples of static electricity. After helping them do this, Christine distributed a worksheet and told them that questions 1 to 7 referred to a video clip they were about to see. She then showed them a five-minute video clip titled 'Static electricity'. This showed how bicycles can be sprayed with less waste of paint when static electricity is used to enable a dry powder paint to be used instead of a conventional wet paint delivered as an aerosol spray.

Christine then replayed the video clip, helping the pupils to appreciate which bits of it related to the questions on the worksheet which they had to answer.

By now it was 10.20 a.m. The girl who had been away at the careers interview returned and the girl who had been involved in the role-play with Rodney left – I presume to go to a careers interview too.

At 10.24 a.m. Christine allowed the girl who had only been present for four minutes to leave on the grounds that it was now the official end of the lesson.

(No hooters were in action because it was the examination season.) Christine then started showing a second, shorter video clip, also about static electricity. This clip finished at 10.26 a.m. and the pupils started to pack up and move towards the door. However, Christine told them that it wasn't the end of the lesson yet and got them to go back to their places. For some reason, the only other girl in the class had also left by now and some of the remaining seven boys complained that it wasn't fair and that the two girls who had been present for the whole of the lesson should get their detentions too.

Christine didn't get involved in a debate about this but simply waited for the boys to be quiet. Indeed, one of the boys told another boy to 'fucking' shut up so they could leave. At 10.29 a.m. Christine let the boys leave.

Peter

Peter didn't know what his Year 9 SATs results were and, though he went upstairs to look for them, couldn't find them. I subsequently found out from the school that he had got a 4 in science. (The levels pupils are 'expected' to get on their SATs are discussed on pp. 46–8. As a rule of thumb, Level 5/6 is the typical expectation on a Year 9 SAT – i.e. for a 14-year-old. Level 4 therefore equates to the performance of a typical 11-year-old, Level 5 to that of a typical 13-year-old and Level 6 to that of a typical 15-year-old. On the same logic, a Level 7 should equate to the performance of a typical 17-year-old, were it the case that all 17-year-olds remained in full-time education and continued to study science.)

Peter left Pasmoor School during the year and I didn't explicitly ask his three science teachers about him when I interviewed them at the end of the year. By coincidence, some two to three weeks after Peter had left Pasmoor School in February, I happened to bump into him at the school to which he had transferred. He seemed well and said he preferred his new school to Pasmoor School. He told me that he was living with his father during the week and seeing his mother at weekends.

I did the end of Year 10 interview (see Tables 5.1 and 5.2) with Peter and his mother. When I asked him how he was finding science he said 'OK' and grinned hugely. I asked why he was grinning and it turned out he wasn't doing science at his new school – something that was clearly news to his mother. I asked what he was doing and he told me English, maths, French, drama and resistant materials. I said that I didn't know much about resistant materials but then it turned out Peter actually managed to get 0 on his Year 10 exam in the subject so I'm not sure he knew more than I did.

Talking of his science days at Pasmoor School, Peter told me that he liked practicals but didn't 'like a lot of sitting down, doing the writing. I liked to get in there straight away . . . I liked Mr Western 'cos we had a laugh but we still done our work. Some of the other teachers . . . you had to sit there and be quiet'. His mother agreed: 'Lessons are more interesting if they're fun'.

Although he had left Pasmoor School, Peter and his mother were happy at

Table 5.1   Questions asked by me of the Year 10 pupils

1 Tell me a bit about what this last year has been like for you.
2 What was work experience like?
3 How have you found the science lessons?
4 Which do you most like out of biology, chemistry, physics? Why?
5 Which do you least like out of biology, chemistry, physics? Why?
6 Tell me about the sort of science teaching you like.
7 Tell me about the sort of science teaching you don't like.

Table 5.2   Questions asked by me of parents of the Year 10 pupils

1 What has this last year been like for [your child]?
2 What has this last year been like for you?

the end of Year 10 interview for me to come and interview them at the end of Year 11. However, when I phoned up to make the usual appointment to see them at the end of Year 11, I found out from Peter's stepfather that he and Peter's mother had split up. I managed to get her new telephone number but the one time I got to speak to her she put the phone down. Thereafter calls were not returned and, after leaving a number of messages on her answerphone, I decided that it was best not to pester her any further.

Rodney

In his Year 9 SATs, Rodney had got a 5 for science. He found Year 10 science 'more interesting than in the past two years' and liked physics the most of the science disciplines ''cos they relate to everyday life'. Perhaps unsurprisingly, given his dyslexia, he didn't like biology, stating that 'there are quite a few hard words to learn'. He didn't like 'textbooks and doing things off the board', preferring practicals and 'if you do something that relates to everyday so that it's easier to remember'.

Roland Newman felt that Rodney 'seems to be maintaining a higher level of concentration, of focus on task, but [is] still operating at a very superficial understanding'. He talked about 'family pressure for Cs' but said that the school was predicting a Grade E or D at GCSE.

Fiona Roberts was very positive about Rodney. 'Academically he's made huge progress since the beginning of the year. Socially he's made huge strides. Personally he's made huge strides . . . he may actually reach his potential . . . so many problems with concentration . . . he's beginning to conquer it. His attitude is so much more positive'. Fiona had taught both Rodney's elder brother and his elder sister so she felt she knew the family well. She talked about how he had a strong family background and about how he was now past 'the worst of adolescence'.

Christine Evans talked about how, when she first arrived, she had found Rodney to have 'a lot of energy, easily distracted. Yeah, but he would always call out a lot of comments . . . involved in a way, you know what I mean . . . almost wants to take over . . . you have to answer him when he asks something'.

George, Martin, Richard and Sue's class

At the beginning of the year, George, Martin, Richard and Sue were taught in a class that had 19 pupils, 8 of whom were girls and 11 of whom were boys. The class's teachers were Katie Toland for biology, Grace Smart for chemistry and Susan de Von for physics.

Grace Smart's teaching

Grace Smart had been at Pasmoor School for four years. Outside of school she liked spending 'time with my family and travelling in the caravan . . . and reading . . . a good newspaper. My favourite thing in the whole world's a good newspaper'. When I asked her about what she was trying to achieve in science lessons she said: 'Well, I think trying to achieve an interest in science because it's all so encompassing . . . the processes of science . . . they can use [the science they learn at school in] problem-solving . . . they can use that throughout their lives . . . you've got to get them through their exam'.

A typical example of one of Grace's lessons was the first one I saw her teach to this group, from 8.45 a.m. to 10.25 a.m. on 15 October. As I signed the school's visitor book, on the way to Grace's lesson, the Receptionist told me that I should be on the payroll. At this point early in the school year, George and Martin hadn't yet been moved up a set. In addition Sue, as quite often seemed to be the case throughout her time at Pasmoor School, was absent, so Richard was the only one of the pupils I had been following since Year 7 who was present along with 10 other boys and 8 girls in a class of 19.

In common with just about all the science teachers at Pasmoor School, Grace devoted considerable energy to chasing up homeworks. This morning, after taking the register, she told them that she was very unimpressed at the 50 per cent who hadn't done their homework. 'Not acceptable in this school . . . I'll be seeing those people after class. Let's make sure this is the last time I have to remind you'.

Grace then began by using questions to get the pupils to recall what they had been doing last time – evidently an experiment about the effect of various factors on the evolution of gas from a reaction between marble chips and acid. Grace drew on the board the graph sketched in Figure 5.1. Continuing her questioning, Grace got the pupils to think about what was going on in

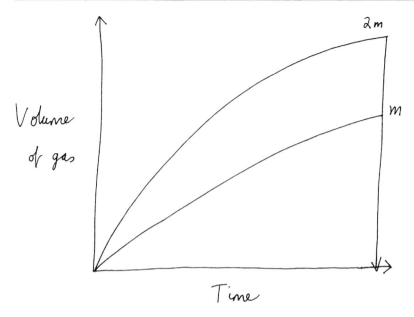

Figure 5.1 First graph drawn on the blackboard by Grace Smart during her Year 10 chemistry lesson on 15 October

terms of particles. She ended up writing on the board that one of the things they could conclude from the graph was:

1 2m acid makes twice the number of successful collisions.

After further questioning she wrote:

2 The 2m reaction is faster – the graph is twice as steep.

Grace emphasized that 'In the exam you're going to have to look at graphs and explain them'. This was the second time in the lesson that she had mentioned the importance of exams. She then told the class that if their graph (i.e. the graph of their own experimental results) didn't look like the graph she had drawn on the board, they should copy the graph from the board into their books.

After spending four minutes going round the class checking how everyone was getting on, Grace wrote on the board:

3 In the 1st 90 seconds, the steepness is twice as much as there are twice as many successful collisions after that _ _ _ _ _ _ _ _ _ _ _ _ _ _

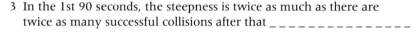

Grace then told them that she wanted them individually to fill in the dotted line. She said that she didn't want them to talk because she wanted their own ideas. A couple of pupils talked and they got ticked off. One of the boys asked if they were going to do another experiment that day.

Four minutes after setting them this task, Grace told them to make sure they used the word 'particles' in their answer. A minute later she wrote on the board

Does Surface Area affect the reaction

and asked for a volunteer from a group who were investigating the effect of the size of the chips. One of the girls came up but the graph she drew had time on the vertical axis. Grace got her to put time on the horizontal axis. The girl wasn't sure what was on the other axis and Grace helped her to see that it should be volume of gas. Between them, Grace and the girl therefore ended up with Figure 5.2.

Grace then got a boy from the same working group as the girl who had helped draw Figure 5.2 to come up and draw what would happen with smaller chips. He drew a curve below the one drawn in Figure 5.2. Grace then rubbed this out and got him to draw it above the curve in Figure 5.2. Grace then asked the pupils what would happen with 2g of large chips compared with 2g of small chips, emphasizing that there were the same number of particles in both. One of the boys attempted an answer and then Grace asked one of the girls whether 2g of chips had the same number of particles as 2g of powder. The girl replied that she thought the powder would react faster.

Grace continued on this theme, trying to get the class to appreciate that initially 2g of powder would react faster but that eventually the same volume of gas would be evolved because there were the same number of particles in 2g of powder and 2g of chips.

By now it was 9.27 a.m., almost halfway through the double lesson. At this point Grace gathered the pupils round the front and started talking to them about hydrogen peroxide. She wrote H_2O_2 on the board and drew:

One of the girls then asked how hydrogen peroxide is made and Grace said she didn't know. Grace then told the pupils that they were going to find out which of two 'identical' black powders made the reaction go faster. She pointed out the hazard symbols for manganese oxide and copper oxide . She told them that she had worked in industry with manganese oxide and it was nasty stuff so she didn't want them snorting it. She then discussed practical arrangements with them. One boy asked what would happen if they did get it (manganese oxide) in their eyes. Grace told them that they wouldn't.

At 9.34 a.m. the pupils began the practical work and Grace did a drawing of the apparatus on the board together with a table for them to fill in. As a heading she had written '$H_2O_2 \rightarrow H_2 + O_2$' and having finished this she came

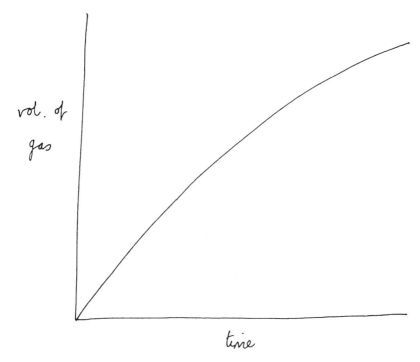

Figure 5.2 Second graph drawn on the blackboard by Grace Smart during her Year 10 chemistry lesson on 15 October

and said to me, rather defensively I felt, 'In case you think that isn't the reaction, I know it isn't'. Trying to sound reassuring I said 'No, no, no'. Grace added 'I want to keep it simple' and I replied 'Yes'. To be honest (a), as far as I knew, $H_2O_2 \rightarrow H_2 + O_2$ was absolutely fine; and (b) I was always extremely conscious, especially when someone hadn't had me in their lessons very often, that it might be quite a strain for a teacher to have me sitting away at the back of the lesson scribbling furiously.

Grace then spent her time going round the pupils as they worked at the practical. For example, one boy feeling the flask said 'Miss – this is getting warm'. Grace replied 'Good, well, it's a chemical reaction, isn't it?' As an aside, it has always fascinated me that almost all female teachers are perennially addressed as 'Miss' irrespective of whether they have children and/or are married. I hesitate to admit it but the rather expensive private school to which I went from the ages of 5 to 12 required – and I promise you this is true – its pupils to address all members of staff as 'Sir', whether they were male or female. This worked perfectly satisfactorily until I left and went to another school. Unsurprisingly, after eight years of such training, there were several occasions at my next school when I inadvertently addressed female teachers as 'Sir'. One new female teacher at the school, in particular, I remember, did not take kindly to this, presuming that I was intending to be rude.

Between 10.00 and 10.09 a.m. Grace got everyone to tidy away their practical apparatus and start working at a worksheet about the rates of chemical reactions. At 10.09 a.m. Grace had a question and answer session with them about the experiment they had just done, getting them to appreciate that for the particular reaction they had been looking at copper oxide was not a catalyst but manganese oxide was. As a conclusion to the experiment Grace dictated 'Manganese oxide catalyses that particular reaction, not necessarily any other'.

The remainder of the lesson consisted of the pupils working away at the worksheet. At the end of the lesson, 10.25 a.m., Grace, as she had said at the beginning of the lesson she would, kept nine of the pupils back because they hadn't done their last homework. The last of these pupils were only allowed to leave at 10.39 a.m. (At Pasmoor School, break, for both pupils and teaching staff, lasted from 10.25 a.m. to 10.45 a.m. and lunch from 12.25 p.m. to 1.10 p.m.) As Grace and I left the lab together she told me that I could write a book on all this.

George

George had got a 5 for science in his Year 9 SATs. He told me that he was 'very pleased' with his SATs results, having also got 5s in English and mathematics.

George had found Year 10 science a lot harder once he had been moved up a set but he was glad he had been moved up. He was absolutely clear that he liked biology the most within science, something he had told me in previous years too. Given that he lived on a farm this didn't surprise me. George had a wonderful collection of plants in his own room and on earlier visits we had had discussions, initiated by him, about whether fish felt pain, about a domestic pear tree of theirs that had a wild branch, about how to catch crayfish and bullheads, and about the behaviour of eels.

Whether George preferred chemistry or physics depended on who was teaching it and whether he found it was clearly explained. When I asked about the sort of science teaching he liked, George answered in terms of how the teacher kept order: 'Teacher being, umm, sort of tough but kind at the same time, like Mr Newman. I always liked Mr Newman . . . 'cos [he was] strict but you could have a laugh'.

Katie Toland commenting about George said 'He seems to me . . . desperately wants to be one of the lads, but he actually wants to do really well and if you separate him from the group . . . that makes him think . . . deep down he wants to succeed'.

Grace Smart felt that George was 'One to watch in case he goes off the rails. Very difficult to keep his focus. Finds it difficult to record written work . . . will often do anything to avoid written work. I think he's clever' – cleverer than the class he was in, she added.

Susan de Von felt that George was 'Very bubbly and enthusiastic. Quite a good scientific knowledge he brings with him. If something grabs his attention, he'll run with it . . . Quite immature. Deep down . . . a clown . . . I like him'.

Martin

Martin wasn't quite sure what his SATs results were but thought he had got a '4 or 5' in science. I found out subsequently from the school that he had got a 5.

Martin preferred biology of the science disciplines – 'I think 'cos the work you're doing is fairly straightforward and you can relate to it . . . you notice it in everyday life; when you do chemistry and physics you don't notice it so much'. Martin was particularly unenthusiastic about chemistry. He talked about how the work was 'generally a lot harder than in the other two subjects . . . you've got to use scientific ideas . . . periodic table . . . I didn't understand a word of it!'

When I asked what sort of science teaching he liked, Martin said 'I think I can understand a lot more if it's practical rather than written . . . quite a lot of the written work . . . I quite enjoy doing the investigations and the experiments'. What he didn't enjoy was 'Written work, copying out of a book'. When I asked him why he didn't like this he answered 'Goes on quite a bit I'd say . . . if it's not explained . . . you might not quite get the gist of things' which made eminent sense.

Katie Toland admitted that she didn't feel she knew Martin very well – which wasn't that surprising as George and he only got moved up halfway through the year. She added 'He almost seems older than the others; does that make sense? He works very hard and has obviously succeeded to move up'.

Grace Smart felt that Martin was 'quite keen to do well but distracted . . . not actually academic; keen to do well . . . doesn't get involved in lessons'.

Susan de Von, though, saw other aspects to Martin, perhaps in part through being, by now, the head of year: 'Delightful . . . quite mature . . . underlying there's a lot more there and I can't quite put my finger on why we're not getting it . . . compliant in lessons . . . quite passive . . . doesn't push himself . . . socially very strong'.

Richard

Richard had got a 6 in his science SAT. Of the three sciences he liked physics the most and chemistry the least. He found it difficult to say why he liked physics the most, though it was probably connected, he felt, with the fact that he got good marks for it. He didn't like chemistry partly because he felt he just couldn't understand 'atoms and ions and all these formulae'. He told me that he liked science teaching when they did new things, rather than having to repeat coursework which they had had to do in chemistry. He also appreciated it when the teachers helped you.

When I had asked Richard at the end of Year 9 what the year had been like for him he immediately replied 'Hard. Hard doing the national tests revising . . .' His mother told me that they had drawn up 'a timetable for revision . . . half past six to ten at night'. In the weeks leading up to the science SAT Richard told me that he spent 'four pages a night on that booklet in science . . . Each page took half an hour or 20 minutes'. (This was the 96-page revision guide I referred to on p. 91.)

At the end of Year 10, Richard talked about all the coursework he had done and the fact that, as a result 'my social life has decreased . . . 'cos of all the revision . . . coursework'. During the summer holidays – i.e. between Year 10 and Year 11 – he was doing at least two hours a day revision using a timetable drawn up by his mother. Richard's mother told me that she had drawn this revision timetable up after consulting with Richard. He needed five Grade Cs in his GCSEs if he was to be able to go to the sixth-form college where he wanted to do his A levels.

Speaking of Richard, Katie Toland said:

> I think he's great. He's quite a loner in that group, umm . . . he's very much on the edge [i.e. of the class] . . . he's a very independent worker who, umm, who I think really could be given extra work to push him on, which is somewhere I've not succeeded, perhaps something to think about for next year . . . if you give him extra work, he does it without dashing if off . . . last lesson that table said 'Come and sit with us' . . . and he was obviously pleased to be asked.

Grace Smart said 'Richard's actually very keen to do well. I get the impression he spends a lot of time on his work at home . . . I get worried he doesn't ask enough questions . . . a lack of confidence, I don't know. Ten out of ten for coursework . . . he listens very well'.

Susan de Von found Richard to be 'very studious, very reserved. Quite a nice sense of humour once you get to know him . . . quite a lot of pressure from home . . . conformist . . . coping not excelling. Has to work quite hard . . . holds back . . . observes rather than taking part'.

Sue

Sue had got a 5 in her science SAT (as well as a 6 in maths and a 5 in English). When I interviewed her at the end of Year 9 she told me that she had wanted to do Triple Award science, i.e. separate biology, chemistry and physics. The reason for this was that, having earlier intended to become an air hostess, she had instead decided to go into hairdressing when she left Pasmoor School. This would involve doing a two-year day release course at one of the local FE colleges. Sue told me that she thought doing the Triple Award course would be useful for hairdressing. I agreed saying that people running hairdressing courses liked one to have done chemistry and biology.

However, at a parents' evening, to which Sue's mother had gone with Sue, Sue had been put off Triple Award science by one of her science teachers who had told her that Triple Award science would involve a lot of science.

At the Year 9 interview I found that the year had been a difficult one for Sue's mother. She now had a new partner who lived 20 miles away. Sue's mother also told me that during Year 9 Sue had had a lot of absences because she didn't want to be at Pasmoor School. I gently asked Sue if she could say a bit more about this. She told me 'I was getting a lot of hassle from people in the year above'. It transpired this was bullying from other girls. Sue told me that this had now cleared up though her mother made reference to some incident only the previous week.

I didn't get to interview Sue at the end of Year 10. On phoning her mother to try and arrange the interview I found out that Sue didn't live there any more, but lived with her father instead. Sue's mother gave me his telephone number but the person who answered the phone told me that he didn't live there. When I eventually spoke to Sue she told me she wasn't keen to be interviewed because she wasn't living at home and because of 'a few problems'. Of course, I acquiesced but I did say that I would be really grateful to interview her at the end of Year 11, whether she would like the interview done at her home, any other home or at school, and she said that would be OK.

For one thing, I was genuinely interested in seeing what Sue would do on leaving school, my having by now a considerable admiration for her perseverance in the face of a number of obvious difficulties in her life. In addition, I was especially keen, if at all possible, not to lose from my original sample of 21 any of the pupils who were still at Pasmoor School.

Katie Toland said that Sue '. . . always tells me that she enjoys the biology and that she enjoys the science . . . I don't think she finds the work very easy. She likes a lot of praise . . . gets fed up with some of the boys . . . She seems older than the boys, a lot more mature'.

Grace Smart told me 'She's really keen. Umm. She's really working well at her potential . . . nearly always managed to get the work done; very mature person . . . My task with Sue is to get the most out of her . . . She works basically to her pace. Maybe I'm being overly harsh on her'.

Susan de Von said of Sue:

Delightful really . . . extremely positive, enthusiastic, conscientious as well . . . very keen to do her best . . . not easy circumstances [at home] having a hard time . . . really wants to do something with her life once she leaves here . . . attendance erratic which ties in with [Susan didn't finish the sentence but I'm sure she knew that I understood that she meant 'home circumstances'] . . . mature approach and gets on with her peers.

Edward, Marc and Paul's class

At the start of Year 10, Edward, Marc and Paul's class had 26 pupils, 8 of whom were girls and 18 of whom were boys. They were taught biology by Emma Harris, chemistry by Stephen Benton and physics by Hannah Thomson.

Emma Harris' teaching

The end of Year 10 interview with Emma was carried out away from Pasmoor School and with her 11-week-old baby at hand. Emma had left Pasmoor School halfway through Year 10, having taken maternity leave. She had asked Pasmoor School if they would extend maternity leave because her husband was going off to Antarctica to work for five months. However, the school had said no. I told her that if ever she wanted a reference I would be happy to write her an extremely positive one.

Emma had come to Pasmoor School in September 1996, having previously taught elsewhere for three years. Outside of school, sports used to be her main hobby – running and skiing in particular. She had also gone on quite a few expeditions and played the oboe semi-professionally. More recently Alexandra (the 11-week-old) was obviously the dominant out-of-school 'interest' though Emma was also in the second year of a Master's course in education.

In her science lessons Emma told me that she was 'trying to convey my enthusiasm for the subject . . . hopefully inspire . . . help them to be confident in themselves . . . so they feel they've done their best'.

An example of one of Emma's lessons was the double lesson I saw her teach on 27 November to this group from 8.45 to 10.25 a.m. Edward, Marc and Paul were all present but for some reason there were only 19 pupils in all, 5 of them being girls and 14 of them boys.

Emma began with a discussion about what they had done last time, during which Edward and Marc both contributed. The class had been looking at how to increase the rate of breakdown of starch when acted on by salivary amylase.

Having completed the review of the previous lesson's work, at 8.56 a.m. Emma wrote 'Enzymes' on the board and told two pupils, one a girl and one a boy, to distribute GCSE biology books. Emma then told the pupils to turn to a particular page and write concise answers to the following questions which she wrote on the board:

1   What is a catalyst?
2   What effect does changing temperature (i.e. increasing and decreasing) have on an enzyme?
3   What effect does changing pH have on an enzyme?
4   What does 'an enzyme is specific' mean?

Emma then spent until 9.17 a.m. going round the groups of pupils helping them as needed. At that point she stopped that exercise and had a four-minute discussion with the class about how food gets to the stomach. She then wrote the following summary on the board and the pupils copied it down:

Digestion and storage in the stomach

Mechanical and chemical digestion takes place in the stomach whilst food is being stored. It is then allowed out in small portions to the next section of the digestive system.

Mechanical breakdown is caused by the muscular stomach wall constantly churning the food.

Chemical breakdown of protein also starts.

While the pupils were finishing writing this, Emma answered a girl's question about why one's stomach churns. Another girl then said that the best time to diet is around exams because you are producing lots of adrenalin.

At 9.28 a.m. Emma gathered the pupils round the front, insisting that Edward, Paul and another boy come closer than they were otherwise going to. She showed them a jar of hydrochloric acid and a beaker of pepsin. Lots of questions and answers ensued including two to Paul which he got wrong, saying that pepsin breaks down starch and that the breakdown of starch begins in the stomach.

Emma then produced a suspension of egg-white, emphasizing that it was cloudy. She put some of it with pepsin in a test-tube. She got the class to realize that this would eventually lead to some of the protein, albumen, in the egg-white breaking down to smaller pieces, and then said 'But I can also tell you that we could sit here for a few years waiting for it to break down'. Emma therefore asked how the speed of the reaction could be increased. One pupil suggested by increasing the temperature; another by adding hydrochloric acid.

Emma agreed with both these suggestions and emphasized that hydrochloric acid doesn't just break down the protein. She added hydrochloric acid and pepsin to some egg-white and got one of the boys to put the test-tubes she had set up into a water bath.

By now it was 9.37 a.m. and Emma told the class a story about stomach ulcers in answer to an earlier question from one of the girls about whether hydrochloric acid in the stomach is dangerous. Another girl then asked why men get more stomach ulcers and Emma answered, emphasizing that it is not just men who get them but that possibly men are more likely to get stressed or that it is because more men work.

At this point the pupils returned to their places and two PGCE (Postgraduate Certificate of Education) students, one male and one female, entered. Emma wrote on the board:

1 What is pepsin and what does it do?
2 Why do you think our stomach makes hydrochloric acid?
3 Will pepsin break down starch? Explain your answer.
4 Why do you think our digestive system (and body) is at around 37°C?

The female PGCE student then walked over to the table at which the five girls were working and started talking with them. Emma walked over to the male PGCE student and explained to him what the class had been doing. She then emphasized to the class that both Mr Simpson and Miss Armstrong were there to help them.

At 9.50 a.m. Emma stopped the class and showed them the results of the demonstration. The test-tube with pepsin and egg-white was still cloudy; the test-tube with acid and egg-white was still cloudy; the test-tube with pepsin, acid and egg-white was beautifully clear. Emma emphasized that this meant that the protein in the egg-white had been broken down by the pepsin in the presence of the acid into small pieces.

At 9.52 a.m. the pupils, with Emma and the two PGCE students helping, went back to answering the four questions on the board. At 9.58 a.m. Emma quietened the pupils and asked them for answers to the fourth question. Edward gave an excellent answer saying that if the temperature was higher, the enzymes would 'deform' and at lower temperatures they would not work as fast. Emma agreed and emphasized that in a test they mustn't say that enzymes 'die' because they are never alive.

At 10.00 a.m. Emma wrote on the board for the pupils to copy down:

<u>Digestion in the duodenum</u>

In the duodenum the digestion of all foods is completed. Carbohydrates, proteins and fats are broken down by enzymes. The pancreas makes these enzymes and pours them into the duodenum.

A liquid called bile is also added from the liver.

At this point, Marc, true to his nature of being able to say things to teachers that other pupils might not be able to, called out to Emma 'You go clubbing with Mr Rogers!' Emma got him to repeat this and then cheerfully said 'I might do!'

While the class finished copying from the board, Emma returned the homework. She briefly summarized what they had seen on the video they watched last time. She then poured some fat into a test-tube followed by some water with the result that the fat floated on top of the water. She told them that in the duodenum the water would contain the enzyme lipase but the water still wouldn't be able to mix with the fat. Emma asked them where bile was stored. Marc suggested the 'pancreas'; someone else gave the correct answer – 'gall bladder'. Emma explained that bile is made from red blood cells and then added washing-up liquid to the test-tube that contained water and fat. She told the class that this was washing-up liquid, not true bile, but that the effect was much the same. Emma shook the test-tube up and got the class to realize that its cloudy appearance was because of the increase in surface area: 'lots of little fat balls; let's call them fat droplets – that's scientific enough'.

At 10.11 a.m. Emma wrote on the board:

1 What does bile do?
2 Why does bile do it?

Emma told the class that they didn't need to use a book and they needed to use 'lipase' in their answer. One minute later she said 'Lots of people are falling asleep. Shall we have a group answer?' There was a chorus of 'Yes' so

Emma asked for a volunteer. One of the girls volunteered and gave a good answer to Question 1 which Emma then dictated. She then, similarly, accepted a contribution from one of the boys for the answer to Question 2.

By now it was 10.15 a.m. and the remaining ten minutes of the lesson were taken up with writing down homework and giving out pupils' coursework marks. The hooter went at 10.25 a.m. and the class were dismissed.

Edward

Edward got a 6 in his science SAT. I somewhat ineptly got in a muddle when preparing my interview schedules for Hannah Thomson and Emma Harris. As a result I don't have any feedback from Hannah Thomson as to how she found Edward and Marc in this group, nor do I have any feedback from Emma Harris as to how she found Jack, Mary and Rebecca in their group. (I do have information about how Emma Harris and Hannah Thomson found Ian and Paul as these two were also in the Triple Award science class which Emma and Hannah taught.)

By Year 10 Edward had decided that he wanted to do photography as a career and he was doing photography GCSE. When I asked him which he liked most out of biology, chemistry and physics, and why, he replied immediately 'Physics. It's the most useful and the chemistry side is not teaching me anything I need to know for my career and most of the chemistry I already know'.

Although he liked Emma Harris, Edward was definite about the fact that he liked biology the least out of the three sciences. When I asked why, he told me that it was 'Boring and I don't like it. Personally I consider it a total waste of time . . . I don't want to know about the insides of a frog'. He also said that he didn't want to know about how to obtain biomass readings by 'sucking' the insides 'out of an animal'. I asked whether he had done this as a practical and, of course, he hadn't. Nor, I very strongly suspect, had he been taught anything about the insides of a frog, but then what is often important in life is people's perceptions of reality rather than reality itself.

Emma Harris remembered Edward as being 'Quite immature . . . I don't think he knows what he's interested in . . . I think he's, if you can generalize, a typical male of that age; needs pushing but resents it . . . his interest needs to be caught but I don't think it was by biology'. But she then added 'I feel guilty generalizing about individuals in this way'.

Stephen Benton felt that Edward 'Still has problems with written work . . . therefore tries to do everything to avoid written work. Wanders off task . . . not without ability but does have this learning disability, learning problem. Absent quite a lot. Quiet sort of boy'.

Marc

Marc couldn't remember how he had done in his SATs and wasn't that keen to go and dig out his report so I said not to worry. I found out subsequently from the school that he had got a 5 in his science SAT. Marc had found Year 10 harder: 'I think I'm in a group that's too advanced for me . . . low marks in the tests'. He, his mother and Hannah Thomson had talked about this and it had been agreed that for Year 11 he would move down a set.

Marc was sure he enjoyed physics the most of the sciences which he put down to the teacher. 'I think it's Miss Thomson probably. I feel she teaches me the best . . . Miss Thomson demonstrates everything'. When I asked him which science he liked the least he replied 'Umm. Chemistry and biology. I don't dislike them but I don't enjoy them the most . . . we don't do many practicals and I enjoy the practical . . . I've probably said that every year! . . . it doesn't sink in as much as the physics does'.

Speaking of Marc, Emma Harris said 'He's very interested in doing something PE-based . . . a terror had come over him . . . exam pressure . . . he so desperately wanted to do well . . . he just crumbled . . . winding himself up for any test . . . I think he was in tears on a few occasions which caught him by surprise . . . very bright, likeable lad who once he's got the confidence back should do really well'.

Stephen Benton told me 'No, umm, I think he's concerned about his progress because he is in a Merit Plus Special group . . . borderline . . . may be moved to the top end of a Merit set. Pleasant. Slowish worker but usually on task. Absent on occasions but nothing of note'.

Paul

Paul got a 6 on his science SAT and had decided to do Triple Award science because he thought that would be appropriate for architecture which he was hoping to study. He preferred science teaching that was 'Not too strict or unstrict; controllable. But can explain properly . . . Teacher not getting stressed'. He liked physics the most of the sciences. This was partly because he thought Miss Thomson was a good teacher and partly because 'it teaches you a lot more you come across and it helps you with the maths and it also coincides with the aircraft'. At this I replied 'I did wonder!' Paul was an extremely keen builder and flier of radio-controlled planes. He had shown me some of them and they looked very impressive with wing-spans of, I would guess, around five feet.

Emma Harris felt that by the time she left, Paul 'was just starting to open up . . . just managing to get smiles from him . . . beginning of the year quite aggressive in his refusal to do work . . . You could see him being interested out of the corner of his eye! . . . seemed quite depressed really'.

For Stephen Benton, Paul was 'Another dreamer there. Needs to be more organized. Needs to work with more urgency. Has problems with the organization of his written work. Quiet. In terms of actual output or ability quite variable: sometimes quite good, sometimes off target. Pleasant enough. Harmless I could say'.

Hannah Thomson told me:

There is more to Paul than meets the eye. Comes across as fairly average ability but I think he's quite sharp beneath it all. I'd say that he lacks a little bit of oomph, a bit of drive. Quite happy to sit back and let life come at him . . . I always get the impression he's just skimming across the surface of things and because of that his sharp ability doesn't come through. In Triple he's consistently getting a C . . . if he had a bit more oomph he could probably get a B. His organization isn't that bad. Homework marks aren't ever brilliant. You get the impression he's doing his homework with the telly on while eating his dinner and chatting on the phone to someone. Presentation poor – handwriting not good and doesn't take much care with . . . underlining titles. I like him. I like all of them . . . grin on his face, happy. He's a plodder.

Burt, Catherine, Nicky and Robert's class

Burt, Catherine, Nicky and Robert were taught in a class that had 27 pupils at the start of the year, 10 of whom were girls and 17 of whom were boys. They had Katie Toland for biology, Grace Smart for chemistry and Susan de Von for physics.

Burt

Burt got a 7 in his science SAT and had found it difficult choosing his options at the end of Year 9, saying 'I'd probably have preferred doing a few more subjects . . . I wouldn't have minded doing Triple science and art'.

Burt said he had found the science lessons in Year 10 'Slightly dull' and didn't have a favourite subject within the three sciences, adding 'I remember falling asleep in chemistry once and being asked a question which I found awfully embarrassing'. He was clear, though, about the sort of science teaching he liked: 'Explaining things, practicals, to the point writing down what it is, rather than having to write down lots of things. Explaining it clearly without contradicting yourself every five minutes'. What he didn't like was science teaching that involved 'Being snappy and squawking at the class every five minutes which actually makes it worse rather than better. Oh, and this sort of public humiliation when you do tests and the person getting the lowest mark has to do something different'.

Katie Toland compared Burt to Robert. 'He's a little more confident that Robert. He will pipe up and tell you what he thinks . . . Quite intelligent . . . I think, but again presentation isn't his biggest [strength] . . . both very difficult individuals to get to know, very difficult'.

For Grace Smart, Burt was 'A little star. He has a lot of difficulty with recording and writing . . . He's done really well because he has genuine recording difficulties in terms of speed . . . polite, helpful . . . quite able in terms of science'.

As was the case for Katie Toland, Susan de Von found herself comparing Burt to Robert – the two of them always sat together. 'Mmm. Not quite as extreme as Robert but a similar world . . . Quite able but not very forthcoming . . . a quiet arrogance as well . . . sometimes when you try to give advice it falls on stony ground . . . not part of the class as a whole . . . sometimes very stubborn'.

Catherine

Catherine got a 5 in her science SAT. She made it clear to me that the science subject she liked most was the one she found easiest. Until Year 10 that had been biology but now she found in biology tests that 'you can't just answer a question, you have to have an explanation, like, with most of them'. I asked if she had any preference between physics and chemistry: 'No, 'cos I find some bits of chemistry hard and some bits of physics hard'.

Catherine was sure that the sort of science teaching she liked 'has to be more than standing up talking otherwise it just goes in one ear and out the other'. I asked if she could give me any examples of good science teaching or a good science teacher. 'Umm. The only example I can think of . . . when the teacher talks about positive and negative electrodes . . . PANIC [i.e. positive = anode; negative = cathode] . . . I always remembered that . . . that's the only example'.

Katie Toland told me that Catherine 'is someone who I think has hugely underachieved this year, big time. She just seems to have lost all enthusiasm . . . homeworks have had to be redone . . . always some gossip to delay [her getting on with her work in class] . . . And if you ask her why it's dropped off, she's very vague and will say "I don't really know"'.

Grace Smart told me that Catherine 'struggles academically to keep up . . . one of the weaker academically in that crowd . . . She doesn't have a natural inclination for the subject . . . doesn't extend herself . . . a delightful personality'.

Reflecting on Catherine, Susan de Von said:

> Mmm. I think a real mixture. I think she doesn't quite know what she wants to be . . . Able . . . a surprising social scene . . . with people not as able as she . . . angst as far as her family are concerned . . . managing to juggle this year better than last year . . . not achieving her full potential . . . has an image problem . . . terrified of being seen as someone with academic success . . . would rather be seen as someone with a bit more street cred.

Nicky

Nicky got a 6 in her science SAT. She had wondered about whether to do Triple Award science because she was intending to become a doctor but, on being told that this wasn't essential for her, had decided to do Double Award instead.

Within science, Nicky's favourite subject was 'Biology, because [it's] about the body, human life . . . I obviously want to become a doctor'. She found chemistry 'boring' and 'Equations in physics so hard! So many to learn'. She added 'I don't like copying from textbooks. I like discussing in a group and doing experiments'.

Nicky had certainly made a positive impression on her teachers. Katie Toland said 'She's great. I think she's lovely. She's a very hard worker, keeps saying she wants to go into medicine, a recurring theme. She'll bend over backwards'.

Grace Smart said 'She's really keen, really keen. She's, she pulls out the stops when she knows what she's doing. She's very social and that can pull her back from being an A* person. Polite, helpful, you can't fault her application . . . really just a well-rounded individual'.

For Susan de Von, Nicky was a 'Star really, I think in every respect. She just [in the sense of 'somehow'] manages to juggle it all . . . very good at sport . . . deputy head girl . . . Setting her sights very high . . . she's a winner . . . she's just got to focus a bit more this last year . . . dilemma of being one of the gang . . . talking about medicine'.

Robert

Robert got a 7 in his science SAT. Part of him at his Year 10 interview was his typical upbeat self, saying that the year outside of school had been 'Not a bit different really; plod on with life'. However, he was positive about how he had found the science lessons saying 'Yeah. They've been all right. Now . . . I've got a lot more friends really, a lot more enjoyable'. He most enjoyed physics within science. At first he said this was because it was 'More practical . . . More experiments' and told me that he didn't like 'pointless writing'. But then, with reference to practicals, he talked about the fact that 'with chemistry and partly biology it's less sort of clear-cut, more sort of debatable as to whether it works or not . . . I prefer it when it's more clear cut'.

When I asked Katie Toland about Robert she laughed and said 'I think he is amazingly shy and very lacking in confidence to the point where he would never choose to speak to me in the lesson . . . he would never choose to move away from Burt. They're inseparable . . . Anything new is very intimidating and he relies heavily on those he's with . . .' She went on to talk about the problems he had with his 'handwriting . . . if there's a computer, that makes a big difference'.

Rather similarly Grace Smart began 'I'm ashamed to admit he's one of the ones I don't know very well . . . Painfully shy. OK one-to-one . . . I've sometimes pounced on him [i.e. with a science question] and he's OK . . . working well so I don't want to embarrass him [i.e. by pouncing on him more often]'.

Susan de Von confirmed the general impression. 'I struggle . . . really, as a teacher and head of year to make contact with Robert . . . very reserved

bordering on withdrawn . . . able . . . seems to operate in his own little bubble
. . . a loner . . . I can't fathom him . . . I'm conscious . . . he can be overlooked'.

Ian, Jack, Mary and Rebecca's class

At the beginning of Year 10, Ian, Jack, Mary and Rebecca's class had 27
pupils, 15 of whom were girls and 12 of whom were boys. They were taught
biology by Emma Harris, chemistry by Stephen Benton and physics by
Hannah Thomson.

Ian

Ian got a 7 on his science SAT. He had chosen to do Triple Award science and
his parents had encouraged him in this, though his mother told me at the end
of Year 9 interview that 'he's now worried he's in with the nerds'.

Ian liked physics the most of the three sciences. He found it difficult to say
why. Partly it was simply that he found it interesting; partly it was that 'it's
more tied in with maths as well'. He didn't like biology as much as chemistry
or physics saying 'I think it's like geography and things – more learning facts
rather than actually working things out'.

Ian told me that he didn't like lessons where the teachers shouted or when
the teacher hadn't got control. When I asked him about the sort of science
teaching he did like, after quite a long pause he replied 'I actually liked the
last lesson in Triple [chemistry] because we were allowed to get on with what
we wanted to do'. This was a lesson in which Ian worked on his own to
improve his coursework grade in science by carrying out part of an investigation that centred on the evolution of gas when hydrochloric acid reacts
with magnesium.

Emma Harris, speaking of Ian, said 'I think, umm, well, a very lovely chap,
very bright, very interested in life and a bit embarrassed about that! . . . if only
he was doing A level he'd really get into it; very organized . . . well balanced
chap really. Pleasure to get to have people like that . . . he could have pushed
himself a bit harder'. She then added that she felt 'uncomfortable' talking
about the pupils and I commented that this was the second time she had said
that.

Stephen Benton said 'He seems a bit more focused now. Has ability. Did a
very good bit of coursework during the year. Trying harder . . . Has to push
himself'.

Hannah Thomson said:

Fairly quiet. Quite reserved. Doesn't get involved very much in lessons
but quietly confident . . . contributes a bit more in Triple. I think Ian is
extremely able. Quick to grasp concepts. The only thing that lets him
down is lack of detail in his written work – typical boy in that respect.

Very organized . . . In the physics he's consistently getting A/A* in the Double Award tests. In Triple Award he's estimated B. That's a minimum. I'm quite sure he'll get an A ultimately. Likes to present his work on computer and puts more detail in. [Pause.] Yeah. I think he's one to watch that he does remain positive or focused.

Jack

Jack wasn't sure what he got in his science SAT but thought it was a Level 7. I found out subsequently from the school that he had indeed got a 7. Jack told me that he found physics the easiest subject of the sciences but didn't really enjoy any of the sciences. He said he preferred biology of the three 'possibly because it's on a Friday afternoon . . . teacher more relaxed. . . . chemistry lessons are a real bore . . . Don't really like chemistry anyway . . . Some of it true to life but it's too complicated, all those different letters . . . physics I can relate more to real life and biology [too]'. He liked science lessons where he got on with the teacher but didn't like it when the teacher 'tries to make a few jokes but they're not funny'.

Stephen Benton said of Jack 'Bit of a dreamer. Has organizational problems . . . I think on report earlier in the year. Not without ability. Lacks self-motivation'.

Hannah Thomson did not feel that Jack had had a good Year 10. 'I think Jack's attitude has been a bit of a problem this year. He doesn't come across as having a particularly positive attitude . . . blatantly rude, like talking when I've been talking. She described his organization as 'a nightmare' and told me, having quickly counted up in her mark book, how often he had forgotten his book and not done his homework. 'Very laid back, doesn't seem to care . . . if I didn't bother to chase him he'd have no notes, do no homework and drop out basically. Ability-wise I don't think he's lacking'.

Mary

Mary got a 6 in her science SAT. When I asked her which she liked most out of biology, chemistry and physics, Mary answered in considerable detail, with reference to the quality of the teaching she felt she was receiving in each of the three disciplines. She was very positive about the teaching she was getting from Hannah Thomson and had got from Emma Harris before she had left. When I asked her about the sort of science teaching she liked she said 'Reasonable amount of discipline, a lot of things written down . . . references to textbooks [and being told] what's the most important thing you need to know'.

Speaking of Mary, Stephen Benton said 'Very diligent. I've had her since Year 7. She's come on considerably. Her spelling has improved. Very conscientious, quite able. Quiet, self-motivated'.

Hannah Thomson said:

Has got to be the most perfectionist I've ever taught! . . . You could publish her book. She must spend hours and hours doing her homework. Incredibly conscientious. I've never taught Mary before. Quite shy at the start of the year . . . After the first half term she got to know me . . . She won't ask in the whole class but when they're working individually she'll always call me over . . . Incredibly well organized, well motivated.

Rebecca

Rebecca got a 7 in her science SAT. She liked both biology and physics. In biology she liked the fact that 'you're working with living things . . . and I liked the topic on ecology . . . physics . . . we did loads of experiments and I enjoyed that'. I asked her why she didn't like chemistry particularly. 'I can't really say . . . I don't know. In some ways it's a lot harder, so much you have to learn but I do like the work'.

Stephen Benton said that Rebecca was a 'Very nice girl, hard working, conscientious, committed, well organized'.

Hannah Thomson said:

She's, well, I like her. Very friendly, polite . . . good sense of humour, seems to enjoy the physics lessons, very able, quite analytical . . . you can see her brain ticking over in discussions, great deal of pride in her written work . . . very mature and sensible. Doesn't need chasing . . . copies up if she's missed a lesson. Homework's generally fine. Could sometimes put a bit more effort in. Coursework . . . absolutely outstanding . . . Estimating A*. An exceptional pupil. In fact, the bit about the homework is that she probably knows she doesn't have to write ten pages like some of them and cuts it down for that reason'.

Ian and Paul's Triple Award class

The year group I was following was the first for which Pasmoor School had run Triple Award science as well as the usual Double Award science. The idea of the course had been strongly supported by certain parents but had proved very hard work for the members of the science department who taught it. The small size of the group – just 12 pupils – meant that the senior management team at Pasmoor School had decided it should be run in consort with the normal Double Award science. What this meant was that the 12 Triple Award pupils went into the normal Double Award lessons for three double lessons (each of 100 minutes) a week and, in addition, had a 50-minute biology lesson with Emma Harris, a 50-minute chemistry lesson with Stephen Benton and a 50-minute physics lesson with Hannah Thomson.

This meant that the 12 Triple Award pupils came from a number of Double Award lessons. In addition, the syllabus for the Double Award and Triple Award didn't mesh especially well. A final difficulty was that there was a far greater range of ability in the Triple Award class than the science department had originally intended.

Despite all this, both Ian and Paul were positive about the Triple Award lessons. Ian said 'The Triple I thought would be harder but it's more of a range of things we do and it's been quite good doing the Triple 'cos I understand the Double better'. He told me that he had thought there would be more than 12 people. I asked him what it had been like, being in a group of 12 and he said 'It's been a really good chance to ask questions'. Paul said that 'In the Double you don't pick up as much as in the Triple'.

Reflections on Year 10

By the end of Year 10 it felt like the pupils were on the last lap of their time at Pasmoor School. In some respects, Year 11 is rather like the second half of GCSE rather than a brand-new year.

Reading through the above accounts of the lessons described in this chapter I am encouraged in that they 'ring true' to me. In addition, they show a wide range of teaching methods used, including practical work, demonstration, class discussion, watching videos, question and answer sessions, copying from the board, use of textbooks, worksheets, dictation, brainstorming and role-play. They also illustrate some of the similarities and differences in approaches between members of the science department. It is also noticeable, that, while some teachers obviously comment on pupils in more detail, there is a high degree of concordance between the views of the various teachers about each individual pupil.

On examining the accounts by the pupils of which disciplines within science they preferred, I am struck by the fact that none of them said they most liked chemistry whereas physics was the outright preference for seven of the pupils and biology for four. Indeed, the only one who came near to saying that chemistry was her favourite was Catherine who said that she preferred chemistry and physics to biology because they were easier. The contrast with the first interview I did with the pupils halfway through Year 7 is striking (see Table 2.1 on page 18).

When I asked pupils to explain why they most liked a particular science discipline there was quite a diversity of answers. In some cases pupils liked a discipline because of out-of-school interests – George with his knowledge of and interest in wildlife, Paul with his love of radio-controlled planes, for example. In a few cases there seemed to be personality reasons for their preferences. Robert, for example, liked the clear-cut nature of physics; Ian liked the fact that in physics he could work things out rather than having to learn a lot of facts. In a number of cases, pupils simply liked the subject they understood the best (e.g. Catherine), that they considered relevant to them (e.g. Martin) and which had (they felt) the best teacher (e.g. Mary).

When I asked pupils to tell me what sort of science teaching they most liked and which they least liked there was quite a lot of agreement. Most of the pupils liked practicals as they had back in Year 7. In addition, they liked teachers who could explain their subject clearly and who had good classroom discipline, but who also had a sense of humour.

Key points

- Teachers used a wide range of teaching methods in science in Year 10, as in all years.
- Pupils varied considerably in their home circumstances.
- By Year 10, of the three science disciplines, chemistry was the least liked by the pupils.
- Sometimes pupils most liked a particular science discipline because of out-of-school interests, sometimes because of aspects of their personality, sometimes because they found it easiest to understand, sometimes because they considered it personally relevant and sometimes because it was particularly well-taught.
- Most of the pupils liked science teachers who used practicals, explained their subject clearly, had good classroom discipline and had a sense of humour.
- Only Ian and Paul of the pupils I was following did Triple Award science. Despite the fact that the course had some problems, due to this year being the first that Pasmoor School had run it, both Ian and Paul were positive about it.

6

Year 11: Revision, exams and moving on

We pack the physical outline of the creature we see with all the
ideas we have already formed about him, and in the complete
picture of him which we compose in our minds those ideas have
certainly the principal place. In the end they come to fill out so
completely the curve of his cheeks, to follow so exactly the line of
his nose, they blend so harmoniously in the sound of his voice
that these seem to be no more than a transparent envelope, so
that each time we see the face or hear the voice it is our own idea
of him which we recognise and to which we listen.

(Proust [1913]1943: 22–3)

The background to Year 11

Pasmoor School is an 11–16 school, so Year 11 was the pupils' last year at the
school. Unsurprisingly, the academic focus of the year was on completing the
various GCSE syllabuses and then revising for the exams. In addition to
watching a good number of science lessons I also, as usual, interviewed the
pupils, their parents and their teachers at the end of the year, after the exams.
Edward's family had spent the summer in Australia, only returning after the
GCSE results were out. I therefore interviewed Edward and his parents after
they had received his GCSE results. The other Year 11 interviews with pupils
and their parents were carried out after the pupils had taken their GCSEs but
before they had got their results. To put the GCSE results of the Pasmoor
pupils in context, Table 6.1 provides some national statistics.

In many cases I found the Year 11 interviews quite moving. I had told all
the parents at the end of the Year 10 interview that the Year 11 interview
would be the last time that I would be interviewing them, though I would
hope to carry on interviewing their daughter/son even after they had left Pasmoor School. In a number of cases during the Year 11 interview the parents
and I found ourselves reminiscing about how the last five years had been for
them and for their family. I was also surprised and, if the truth be known,

Table 6.1   National performance in GCSEs for selected subjects in England and Wales in June 1999

Subject	%A*	%A	%B	%C	%D	%E	%F	%G	%U
Double Award science	3.9	7.8	12.8	26.3	21.7	14.9	8.2	2.9	1.4
Biology	13.5	25.0	27.3	20.6	8.8	3.0	0.8	0.2	0.7
Chemistry	15.2	25.8	25.8	20.8	8.2	2.6	0.8	0.2	0.6
Physics	18.1	24.4	24.4	20.6	8.4	2.4	0.8	0.2	0.7
All subjects	4.4	10.8	16.9	23.7	18.7	12.8	7.5	3.4	2.0

rather touched at the number of parents who said they would miss my coming. But then I suppose most of us appreciate someone who takes a genuine interest in us and our families.

I also found it increasingly difficult, as I wrote the later chapters of this book, deciding what to leave out! I suppose a book could be written from my notes about each of the pupils I was following over the five years I had studied them. During that time they had developed from young schoolgirls and schoolboys just out of primary school into young women and men who had reached the school leaving age and were about to begin another major phase of their lives.

In this chapter I mainly concentrate on what the 15 pupils who were still at Pasmoor School (out of the original 21 with whom I started) were intending to do now that they were leaving the school. Over the five years I had asked various questions, of both pupils and parents, about their hopes on leaving Pasmoor School (see Table 6.2) and the answers to these questions are summarized here.

In this chapter I also describe a lesson of Jenny Morrison's, the teacher who came to Pasmoor School when Emma Harris left. Because the lessons I described in Chapter 5 (Year 10) were all Double Award lessons, the one of Jenny's that I'll describe will be a Triple Award lesson.

The one pupil present in Year 10 who did not return for Year 11 was Rodney. I went and interviewed him, and his mother, at the end of Year 11 as usual. He had spent the year instead at an independent sixth-form college studying for his GCSEs and was positive about it. He liked the fact that he was doing fewer subjects – just five, including science – and the fact that there were quite a few students there in their twenties so that the atmosphere felt 'far more grown up'.

When I asked Rodney's parents back in Year 7 what their hopes were for him, they had both felt that he would do well, despite his dyslexia. His mother had described him as a 'survivor' and his father had talked about how, if only he could, Rodney would probably leave school at 14. At the Year 9 interview Rodney told me that 'I want to try to get an apprenticeship as a boat-builder'

Table 6.2   Questions posed by me to pupils and parents about their hopes on leaving Pasmoor School

Year	Interviewees	Question
7 (2nd visit)	Parents	What are your hopes for [your child] for the future?
9	Pupils	What would you like to do when you leave Pasmoor School?
9	Parents	What are your hopes for [your child] for the future?
11	Pupils	What are you going to do now that you have left Pasmoor School?
11	Parents	How are you feeling about what [your child] is intending to go on to do now that (s)he has left Pasmoor School?

and his mother talked about wanting 'him to have some sort of creative job . . . job satisfaction . . . to be happy . . . reasonable standard of living'. At his Year 11 interview, Rodney told me that he wanted to go into boat-building and while that hadn't yet got fully sorted out, getting onto such a course didn't depend on his GCSE grades. His mother was positive about such a course 'though I don't think he will be in boat-building all his life'.

George, Martin, Richard and Sue's class

George, Martin, Richard and Sue continued to be taught biology by Katie Toland, chemistry by Grace Smart and physics by Susan de Von.

George

When I drove up to their farmhouse on my Year 11 visit, Jess, a beautiful black labrador, greeted me as he always did. He had been just 8 months old on my first visit but was now a 5-year-old and perhaps a shade less sleek. It was in the second half of August. My interviews with George and his parents inevitably took place later in the summer than most others so that his father could finish getting the harvest in.

Since back in Year 7, and I am sure long before then, George had wanted eventually to take over the farm his father worked as a tenant farmer as his own father had taken it over from his father before him. Both George's parents wanted him to do well in his studies. In Year 7 his mother commented 'I think one always wants one's children to do better than one did oneself – my mother did' while his father talked about his worries concerning the future of small farms and whether there might not even be a farm for George to take over.

The aim of going into farming remained constant throughout the five years I had known George. In Year 10 he had done his work experience at a Cambridge firm where he learned about hydroculture for growing plants. He had really enjoyed his work experience and told me that he 'got paid in the end because they said I'd worked really well . . . better than school'. Indeed, George had got a holiday job there after finishing at Pasmoor School.

George got two Grade Cs in his science GCSEs and a B, two Es, three Fs and a G in his other GCSEs. In September he was starting what he wanted to do, namely a B.Tech. 1st diploma in horticulture at an agricultural college.

Martin

On my second Year 7 visit, Martin's father told me that his main aspiration for his son was 'really and truly, if he's happy'. Two years later, Martin wasn't sure what he wanted to do on leaving school: 'I don't know. Either going into coaching or something like that. I don't know. It depends what suits me. I dunno. I'll probably change my mind a couple of times before Year 11'. At that time his father hoped he might play first-class cricket. His mother's more modest ambitions were '. . . just hope he gets on all right . . . doesn't get into trouble'.

Martin did his work experience in a sports shop and really enjoyed it. When I interviewed him at the end of Year 11 he was hoping to go to sixth-form college to do A levels in PE, maths and DT (design technology). He needed five Grade Cs for this. In fact he ended up getting two Grade Cs in his science GCSEs and a B, three Cs, a D and two Es in his others.

Richard

When I asked Richard's parents in Year 7 what their hopes were for him, his father replied 'Like any parents, to do better than we did. Neither of us went to university. If he's able to, we'll support him'. His mother then said 'So long as he's happy' and his father added 'Ideally we just want the best for him that he can possibly achieve'.

The Year 9 parents' interview was done with Richard's mother on her own and she answered the question about her hopes for Richard's future by smiling and saying 'My hopes for Richard are completely different to his father's! My hopes for him are to be happy'. She went on to say that Richard's father was 'really keen for him to go to university . . . Richard would like to go into banking'.

Richard had done his work experience at a building society and described it as 'Brilliant. Absolutely brilliant . . . Serving customers the second day!' By the end of Year 11 he was hoping to go to sixth-form college and do A levels in geography and IT [information technology] and either A level business studies or AS/B Tech. mathematics. Richard told me this was provided he got the necessary five Grade Cs. His parents were very pleased at the prospect of him going to sixth-form college. In fact he got two Cs in science, an A in IT, five other Cs and two Ds.

Sue

As described earlier (see p. 110), Sue was intending in Year 9 to go into hair-dressing and had wanted to take Triple Award science for that reason. When I asked Sue's mother in Year 9 what her hopes were for Sue's future she replied 'Well, I do hope that she does really well, especially when she comes to her last year at college. Well, having said that, I think she will shock or surprise everyone . . . Although Sue wants to be a hairdresser, I think she undermines herself because I think she could do better'.

I conducted the Year 11 interview with Sue in her grandmother's home, where she was now living. The last two years had not been easy ones for Sue. As she put it 'It wasn't all a bed of roses'. Her mother had remarried but it hadn't worked out and they were now divorcing. Sue had never got on with her stepfather and so she had lived apart from her mother for those two years.

At the time of the interview Sue was working in a hairdressing salon but there were transport difficulties in getting there. The problem was that if she remained at the salon and did the course to be a qualified hairdresser she would have to spend two years spending most of her income on bus fares. That, combined with the fact that she had to pay rent and that her mother was no longer able to claim for her now that she had left school, meant that she was about to abandon hairdressing and try to get an office job.

Sue got DD in her science GCSEs and a C, five Ds and two Es in her other GCSEs.

Marc's class

Marc had moved down a set at the end of Year 10 and was now in a class who were taught biology by Jenny Morrison, chemistry by Stephen Benton and physics by Hannah Thomson.

Marc

At the Year 7 interview when I asked about his mother's and his stepfather's hopes for the future for him, Marc's mother said 'I used to say that I wish he would join the army at 4! . . . I hope he achieves'. His stepfather said 'I hope he develops a good understanding of himself. I hope he develops a tolerance towards other people. I hope he gets into top set maths otherwise we're in real trouble. I hope he continues with his attitude that life is fun even when it's serious . . . never feeling he's failed at anything because you can't'.

On my Year 9 visit Marc talked about how he would like to play football after leaving school. I explored with him whether there was a possibility of that and he said 'I doubt it . . . not sure otherwise'. His mother said 'Well, I hope that he'll be happy. I hope he'll realize the need to work hard to be happy because it'll open up more chances. Long-term I hope he'll be a success and that success can only be measured by him'. Marc's stepfather added '. . . that he works towards exploiting his abilities so that he not only becomes a better person but works towards influencing people'.

After leaving Pasmoor School Marc was going to go to a local college to do the national diploma in the uniformed services. This would lead on to him becoming a policeman or fireman or going into the army, navy, air force or coastguard. His mother said she was 'absolutely thrilled . . . I actually think it's a course that'll suit him . . . very practical . . . opportunities to pursue his sporting interests too . . . I think it'll maintain his interest'. She also said that she thought eventually 'he'll go into sales'. Marc had done his work experience in retail and had really enjoyed it.

Marc got two Cs in his science GCSEs and four Cs and five Ds in his other GCSEs. When I phoned him up and congratulated him he told me that he was really pleased and was going out to celebrate later that evening.

Edward, Jack and Paul's class

Jack had moved down a set at the end of Year 10 and was now in the class with Edward and Paul that was taught biology by Jenny Morrison, chemistry by Stephen Benton and physics by Hannah Thomson.

Edward

Back in Year 7 when I asked Edward's mother what her hopes were for Edward for the future (see p. 32) she replied: 'I'd like him to be a confident adult and obviously to be able to get a job at the end of it. He hopes to go into computing which is what his father does. At one point he wanted to be a vet but obviously that's out of the question. I'd like him to go to university . . . Be happy . . . Biggest worry is GCSEs . . . getting him more time perhaps'. Edward's father said 'I suppose the main one would have to be that he's happy and in order to be that he'll have to be successful in one way or another'.

Edward's answer at the Year 9 interview as to what he would like to do when he left Pasmoor School took a different tack from most pupils: 'Take it as it comes. As I see it, you can have your heart and mind set on something but not actually get it so take what you can get and when you can get what you want, get it'. On the same visit Edward's father answered the question by saying 'Health and happiness' and his mother said 'For me, for him to be independent and leave home! . . . We've never imposed a career on him like "Ooh, he must be a lawyer". We've stood back from that. He'll have to make his own decisions'.

Six months before he left Pasmoor School, Edward's parents had paid for someone to assess him. They were informed that he was in the top 1 per cent of people intellectually. At this point, they told me, the 'teachers woke up to the fact that he wasn't just dreaming'. Edward too was pretty unimpressed with how long it had taken before Pasmoor School had acknowledged his dyslexia – which his mother had talked to me about in Year 7. As Edward put it '. . . three years for the school to realize . . . this woman takes five minutes!'

Edward didn't do as well in his GCSEs as he had hoped. He had got two Cs in his science GCSEs, an A* in photography, one other C, three Ds and two Es. Fortunately, although the sixth-form college to which he wanted to go had originally stipulated five Grade Cs, the A* in photography with three Cs proved sufficient to let him go there to take photography and media studies at A level, electronics at GCSE and to retake English language at GCSE.

Jack

On my Year 7 visit, when I asked Jack's parents about their hopes for him for the future, his father had said 'I don't have a sort of line laid out. Obviously I'd like him to develop his talents. Fundamentally I'd like him to be happy. That's the goal. Anything he's good at he should have a chance at . . . It'll be very interesting seeing what he does. I'd like him to go to university, but not necessarily immediately'. Jack's mother added 'It wouldn't be any good pushing him in the wrong direction. I think Jack's lucky because he's generally bright and can keep his end up. He does sometimes get frustrated if he comes up against things he has to work at'.

When I asked him at the end of Year 9 what he wanted to do on leaving Pasmoor School Jack wasn't sure but raised the possibility of going to college and doing music, either at college or outside of it. His parents' hopes for him echoed those expressed two years earlier. His mother said 'He's lucky because he's quite talented and generally bright and gets a reasonable amount of support at home . . . fulfil himself . . . he is unsure of himself'. His father added '. . . hope he ends up doing something in an intensive way'.

On finishing at Pasmoor School, Jack told me that he was intending to go to sixth-form college and do A levels in media studies, English and either computing or music technology. In fact he got two Bs in his science GCSEs, four As, two other Bs, a C and a D.

Paul

In Year 7, in answer to my question 'What are your hopes for Paul for the future?', Paul's mother had replied 'I want him to do whatever he's happy at doing. I just feel the Lord's got their lives planned . . . It would be nice if they went to university . . . but I'd just like them to be happy at what they're doing . . . All we really want is for the kids to be happy going to Church' (see p. 39).

Two years later, Paul's mother answered the same question by saying 'I want him to aim for as high as he is capable of going – there's no point aiming for something you know you can't get'. On the same visit Paul told me that he wanted to study architecture though he realized that he would 'need high grades' and that there was 'a high dropout rate'.

By Year 11 Paul had decided to do a GNVQ in built environment at sixth form college. The idea was that if he got four or five grade Cs he could do the advanced GNVQ in this; if he didn't get those grades he would first do the one-year intermediate GNVQ in built environment and then go on to the advanced course. Paul told me 'I've got plans for being an architect technician but I'm sort of getting second or third thoughts. I think I prefer building or carpentry'.

His mother, who was in earshot, made sort of disagreeing-with-this-being-a-good-idea noises at this point. When I asked her what she felt about what Paul was going on to study she said 'Well, I'm looking forward to the future. I really am hoping he's done well in his exams . . . on the other hand, the Lord's got his hands on Paul . . . whatever the Lord's got planned will happen if Paul will allow that . . . I'm not going to go up to the school and say that! . . . it's got to be what he's happy doing'.

In the event, Paul (who was doing Triple Award science) got a C in biology, a D in chemistry, a C in physics, five other Ds and an F. As a result he was heading off to college to do the intermediate built environment course and would probably retake English and maths at GCSE in each of which he had got a D.

Burt, Catherine, Nicky and Robert's class

Burt, Catherine, Nicky and Robert continued to be taught biology by Katie Toland, chemistry by Grace Smart and physics by Susan de Von.

Burt

When, in Year 7, I asked Burt's mother what her hopes were for him she had replied 'Oh dear! It's obviously dangerous to hope. To put goals in their way. I think it's a balance between temperament, ability and interest, all three. [Pause.] At the moment my worry is he's such a bad speller' (see p. 30). She had then added 'He seems to be good at maths, so we'll see whether he ends up in the scientific way . . . I would hope he would go on to college 'cos the best thing you can do is to give education to your children . . . but I don't know where his future lies . . . where jobs come from and how you keep yourself alive'.

At the Year 9 interview Burt, when I asked him what he would like to do on leaving Pasmoor School replied 'Umm. Not too certain but something to do with design – graphic design maybe'. His mother, who hadn't been present when I was interviewing Burt, answered my question about her hopes for him in the future by saying 'Oh goodness! Complicated. Well, I'd like him to go on and do A levels and go to college. You'd want him obviously to do a course he's interested in . . . beyond that, the world seems so uncertain, I'm not sure what career . . . computer graphics might be something . . . He did say he didn't want to be an accountant'.

By Year 11 Burt was hoping to go to sixth-form college to do A levels in computing, maths and physics. I asked how he was feeling about doing those and he replied 'A little bit daunting because all of them seem archaic. Should have done performing arts and drama'. I asked 'So what did lead you to do the three?' and he answered 'Because I'm interested in them and they fit together very well'.

When I asked Burt's mother how she felt about what he was intending to do on leaving Pasmoor School she replied 'I hope he's all right 'cos he's dyslexic'. She went on to tell me how Pasmoor School had said that he could not have extra time for his GCSEs. As a result his parents had paid for an educational psychologist to do various tests and, in consequence, he had been given extra time for his GCSEs. The tests had revealed that his reading and spelling were typical for a 12- to 13-year-old whereas his IQ was very high. In addition he had a very limited short-term memory. Burt's mother wondered about the importance of inheritance in dyslexia, saying that she was bad at spelling but not as bad as Burt.

In fact Burt got two As in his science GCSEs and another A, four Bs, two Cs and a D in his other GCSEs.

Catherine

In Year 7 Catherine's mother expressed her hopes for her daughter by saying 'Umm. I hope she'll be happy in whatever she chooses to do. I hope she'll go on to further education and develop a career for herself so she'll be an independent sort of person. That's it really'. Two years later the same question was answered similarly: 'Well, I hope she'll go into further education and enjoy it, umm, the experience of university is something not to be missed and that she'll be happy and get into a career she really enjoys. But only if that's what she wants . . . I don't want her to think that just because her sisters have gone to university she has to'.

In Year 9 Catherine said she thought she would 'like to go to sixth-form college . . . I'm thinking I want to be a social worker'. By Year 11 she was intending to go to sixth-form college and do A levels in psychology, sociology and business studies. I asked her how she was feeling about that and she said she was 'looking forward to it'. Her mother was positive about this and talked about how Catherine 'seemed to have matured in the last year . . . back to the Catherine we knew and loved'.

In fact Catherine got two Grade Cs in her science GCSEs and two Bs and six Cs in her other subjects.

Nicky

At the second Year 7 interview, in Nicky's presence, her parents alternated in their answers when I asked them about their hopes for her. Nicky's father: 'Well, we hope she never grows up! . . . All parents do, I hope she'll be happy'. Nicky's mother: 'I hope she'll use the brain she has. At the moment she wants to be a paramedic'. Nicky's father: 'She's wanted to be that for over a year now'. Nicky's mother: 'It's something I'd like one of the children to do because it's something I'd always wanted to do, though I know it isn't a good reason for wanting one's child to do something'. Nicky's father: 'She'll do well in something with communication. I hope she won't move too far away'. Nicky (teasingly): 'I'm thinking of moving to Florida!'

At the Year 9 interview when I asked Nicky what she would like to do when she left Pasmoor School she immediately responded 'Doctor' and then 'I'd like to go into the sixth form and study all the sciences and the maths'. She then asked me if she had to do chemistry to become a doctor and I answered carefully to the best of my ability (the short answer is 'yes') but also said that she would get some careers advice the following year or possibly at the beginning of Year 11.

When I asked Nicky's parents at the Year 9 interview, in Nicky's presence as was the case in Year 7, what their hopes were for her in the future the conversation went as follows. Nicky's mother: 'She becomes a doctor'. Nicky's father: 'Yes'. Nicky's mother: 'But if it doesn't happen, so long as she's,' Nicky: 'Rich!', Nicky's mother: 'fulfilled'. Nicky's father then told me that the family had been down to London and when they went past the Ritz, Nicky had said that she would go there when she became a doctor! We all laughed and I said that my father was a doctor but I hadn't ever been to the Ritz.

Nicky had done her Year 10 work experience at the vet's surgery in the village where she lived. I wasn't surprised to hear that she 'loved it'. She told me how she had been 'introduced to everyone . . . did injections . . . took X-rays, sterilized equipment'.

On asking Nicky at the end of Year 11 what she was going to do I wasn't surprised that she was intending to do A levels at sixth-form college but her choice of subjects – human biology, sociology and sports science – were not what I had been expecting her to say. In addition to these she would be doing general studies within which she could do such courses as sports leadership, first aid and fitness.

When I asked Nicky's parents, again in Nicky's presence, how they felt about what she was intending to do now that she was leaving Pasmoor School, her mother said 'Very happy' and her father 'pleased she's going to do something she can enjoy'. However, they also told me about how one of the representatives from the various local sixth-form and other FE colleges had put Nicky off becoming a doctor. When Nicky had told him she wanted to become a doctor he had shaken his head and started to tell her about one of their students who hadn't managed to get to read medicine even though he had four grade As (i.e. at A level). He had also told Nicky that that student had had an 'Asian name' which had further put Nicky off as her family name was also not an English one. Finally, Nicky pointed out to me, 'I don't like chemistry' though her mother rejoined 'You're good at it!'

Nicky got two Grade As in her science GCSEs, three other As, a B and two Cs.

Robert

When I asked Robert's mother in Year 7 about her hopes for him in the future she said 'Oh Gosh. Umm. I don't know. I suppose that, err, he keeps doing as well at school so that when he decides to work (I'm sure this meant eventual paid employment not working at school) he does well'. She then added something about the possibility of his going to university, though I didn't catch the exact words, and said 'enough to get a job, and that he enjoys, and gets on reasonably with people, and consequently be happy, you know'.

Two years later Robert said of his wishes on leaving Pasmoor School 'Well, I wanted to, like, go to college so I can do something to do with electronics or computer software'. His father said 'I hope he just uses the assets he's got . . . I'd be disappointed if he didn't go into further education'. His mother told me that when Robert had heard the announcement about Microsoft coming to Cambridge he had said 'My ambition is to get a job there'. His father said that Robert knew how to add memory to computers and his parents then told me how Robert had helped his father with his price list. I asked them to show me and they produced a computer-generated catalogue for his father's business. This had all the prices of heating equipment along with scanned pictures which Robert had done. It looked really rather professional and, impressed, I joked about how maybe Robert could do work experience with them next year.

In fact Robert got his first choice for work experience, working in a shop that sold electrical equipment, but he found it 'Very boring . . . nothing for us to do . . . just standing about and not much else really'.

By the end of Year 11, Robert was hoping to go to sixth-form college to do A levels in maths, computing and electronics. His mother said she was 'Very proud; very pleased' at this prospect. His father said 'Yes. I didn't think when he started Pasmoor School' and his mother finished the sentence, saying 'how well he'd do'.

Robert got two Grade As in his science GCSEs, another A, two Bs, three Cs, two Ds and an E.

Ian, Mary and Rebecca's class

Ian, Mary and Rebecca continued to be taught biology by Jenny Morrison, chemistry by Stephen Benton and physics by Hannah Thomson.

Ian

Back in Year 7, when I asked Ian's parents what their hopes were for him, his father, who has a Masters degree in astronomy and works in research and development in computer graphics, said 'I myself see a lot of myself in Ian so it's a rather biased view! . . . So I would like to see him do well in science. I feel maths is very important, so I'm pleased he's doing well in maths. So I'd like him to get on well in that. I'd like to see him become less shy'. His mother then added 'and more confident . . . Like all parents a bit worrying, the uncertainty, the worry of falling between stools in the school system and nobody noticing' (see p. 33).

On my Year 9 visit, Ian's mother answered the same question I had asked at Year 7 by talking about how she and her husband didn't want to pressurize Ian or his brother and then added, with a laugh, 'obviously we'd like them both to do wonderfully at university!' On the same visit, Ian told me that he would like to 'Do my A levels. Then, if I can, go to university, then work with computers or something'.

By the end of Year 11 Ian knew that he was going to sixth-form college to do A levels in physics, chemistry and double maths. I told him that that was what I had done and he told me that it was 'What my brother's doing – and my Dad did single maths, physics and chemistry!' Ian's mother was 'very positive' about this but added that it was 'very difficult to have just a year between' Ian and his elder brother doing the same subjects at the same sixth-form college.

Ian (who was doing Triple Award science) got a B in his biology CGSE, an A in his chemistry, an A* in his physics, another A*, two other As, three other Bs and two Cs. When I phoned up the day the results came out Ian wasn't in so I spoke with his mother. She told me that he had been disappointed with the B in biology and couldn't understand how he had only got an A (rather than an A*) in IT. We chatted for quite a bit about this, me saying that I really did hope that it didn't put a damper on things and that objectively they were a most impressive set of results. His mother then sounded more cheerful. She said she'd pass the message on to Ian and added that she was sorry he wasn't in to hear it from me for himself.

Mary

In Year 7 Mary's mother and stepfather talked about their hopes for Mary thus. Mary's mother: 'Not in any order of preference . . . fulfil her potential'. Mary's stepfather: '. . . get to university and do a job she feels happy with . . . become a professional something or other'. Mary's mother: 'She's talked about going to university and . . . above all I'd like her to be happy whatever she does'. Mary's stepfather: 'That's right'. Mary's mother: 'As she's so competitive, she'd have to be challenged'. Mary's stepfather: 'Sees herself as having six children . . . loves babies'. Mary's mother: 'Has a knack with babies'.

On my Year 9 visit Mary herself said that after leaving Pasmoor School she wanted 'probably something to do with medicine . . . depends what grades I get'. Mary's parents spoke in similar terms to those they employed two years earlier. Mary's stepfather: 'I'd like her to do something that she's really interested in . . . I want her to achieve what she wants to achieve . . . I'd like it to be one of the professions . . . certainly I'd like her to go to university'. Mary's mother: 'She's actually motivated to go to university . . . I just want her to achieve her potential and do something she's happy at . . . sometimes they have to learn for themselves'.

Mary had been going to do her Year 10 work experience at a leading infertility clinic but then they had cancelled at short notice on the grounds they were doing some building work. Her parents rushed round and sorted out a placement for her at a GP's (general practitioners) surgery and Mary had found that 'Good fun'. She had done some receptionist's work, met patients and had done a baby clinic in the pharmacy.

On leaving Pasmoor School Mary was hoping to go to sixth-form college to do A levels in chemistry, biology and maths and an 'AS' level in art. I asked her what led her to choose these and she replied 'Maths I just like. Art I just like as well . . . Chemistry 'cos you need it. If I had me a choice, I wouldn't do it. Biology 'cos I want to do medicine or something in research. I'd have liked to take physics but in the long-term it wasn't what I wanted to do'. She told me that 'If I don't get the grades, I'll do arts [i.e. humanities]'.

When I asked her parents, in Mary's presence, how they felt about what she was hoping to do her stepfather light-heartedly said 'Disaster doing sciences! She's obviously very keen to do what she wants to do . . . hope the results are OK . . . she's on her own; we know nothing about maths'. Her mother then said to her '. . . it's your choice . . . we don't want you to do too much'. Her mother then talked about how the work experience had given Mary an idea of what being a doctor might be like.

Mary got two As for her science GCSEs, one A*, five other As and two Bs.

Rebecca

When I asked Rebecca's parents, in her presence, on my second Year 7 visit what their hopes for Rebecca were, her father said to his wife 'Well, I know what mine are! You go first'. Rebecca's mother then began 'What do I hope? I hope she'll be happy. She'll do what she wants to do'. At this point Rebecca interjected and said she would like a 'kitten and get my ears pierced and my hair green'. Her father cheerfully told her that when she left home she could do what she liked. Rebecca's mother then asked her husband what he was going to say and he replied 'Well obviously I'd like her to go to university'.

On my Year 9 visit when I asked Rebecca what she would like to do when she left Pasmoor School she said 'Haven't got a clue!' and laughed, then continued 'I'd really like to do something with people but not social services . . . I was thinking of retail management or the catering side of retail management'. On the same visit Rebecca's mother told me that she hoped Rebecca would have 'a career that she enjoys but one that also will be financially good . . . I think she's bright enough to do almost anything she wants to do . . . and she's becoming assertive; quite a forceful character!'

Rebecca had done her work experience in a large store and 'really enjoyed it' though 'the work wasn't incredibly exciting'. On leaving Pasmoor School she was going to a sixth-form college to take A levels in 'sociology, business studies and I think it's English language and AS level in photography'. Her mother was 'very happy about it . . . I think she's doing what she wants to do . . . it doesn't worry me that she hasn't got very clear ideas about what she wants to do . . . she wants to go to university'. Her father talked about how 'she's aiming towards people rather than sciences . . . she'll talk to anyone'.

Rebecca got two As in her science GCSEs, an A*, four other As and three Bs.

Ian and Paul's Triple Award class

The members of the Triple Award class continued to be taught two-thirds of their lessons in Double Award time and, in addition, had weekly single lessons from Jenny Morrison for biology, Stephen Benton for chemistry and Hannah Thomson for physics.

Jenny Morrison's teaching

Jenny Morrison had arrived part-way through Year 10 when Emma Harris left. Initially, therefore, she had only been appointed on a maternity post. She then got an extension of her contract to Christmas in Year 11. At that point she and Katie Toland as well as a number of external candidates applied for the post of head of biology at Pasmoor School. Katie was appointed. Subsequently, Jenny, again in the face of external candidates, was successful in getting a permanent post as a member of the science department.

When I enquired as to her out-of-school interests, she told me that she was a foster carer and that the previous weekend had been the first weekend in eight that she hadn't been looking after children, so she had gone camping. Other interests included 'gardening, anything outside rather than being inside all the time, cycling'.

I asked about what she was trying to achieve in science lessons and she replied 'Oh dear, sounds like when the jargon comes out! I'm trying to impart some understanding, some positive knowledge but I'm trying to foster their imagination, to find out for themselves, which is what particularly doesn't work in a Triple lesson because they're so short. I'd be happier if they came across liking and wanting to read about science rather than passing their exams'.

As an example of one of Jenny's lessons, and because it was a revision lesson, I'll describe the last lesson I saw her teach to the Triple Award class on 6 May from 8.45 to 9.35 a.m. The majority of the science lessons the pupils at Pasmoor School had for their last four to six weeks of the year were revision lessons.

Both Ian and Paul were present but one girl was absent, so there were 11 pupils in the class, 3 girls and 8 boys. After taking the register, Jenny told the pupils to get out their exercise books. She reminded them that last week they had said they wanted to do some revision on nerves so would they please look up 'nerves' in the textbook she was now giving out. Jenny then spent two minutes clarifying for them the extra bits in the Triple Award syllabus on nerves relative to the Double Award syllabus. She told them which questions in the textbook she would also like them to do.

At 8.52 a.m. the pupils started work on this. At 8.55 a.m. Jenny ticked off one of the boys for not doing some homework and another boy for just writing on his exercise book. Jenny moved this latter boy to the table on which the three girls were sitting. She then told the whole class that they would have no formal homework for these last two weeks at school. Instead they should 'revise'.

At 8.58 a.m. Jenny ticked off two other boys for being silly, ticked off the boy she had moved and told one of the girls 'Please make sure that [the boy she had moved] works'. At 9.00 a.m. Jenny chatted socially with the three girls. Between them they got onto the topic of someone at school who has a glass eye.

At 9.07 a.m. Jenny cajoled Ian and two other boys to do more work. At 9.15 a.m. Jenny spent a minute chatting with these three pupils about the different types of GCSE revision books and about revision generally.

At 9.16 a.m. Jenny said to the boy whom she had moved 'will you stop ruining the ladies' concentration?' and at 9.28 a.m. one of the boys, seeing this boy chatting with the three girls said 'such a ladies' man; such a stud'.

At 9.32 a.m. Jenny talked to the whole group about the different revision techniques she had found, going round the group and telling them 'Do not rely simply on reading'.

At 9.35 a.m. Jenny let the pupils pack up and two minutes later she dismissed everyone except the boy she had moved and one other boy. She told these two that she was not content just to let them waste opportunities. 'Why should I have to chase after you to get you your GCSE? . . . You're going to waste this opportunity badly'. After two minutes of this, the two boys were dismissed.

Table 6.3   Analysis, by pupil, of whether or not they were going on to study science after leaving Pasmoor School with the approximate percentage of time that they would be spending on science

Pupil	Science-related subjects they were going on to study	Approximate % of their immediate study that would be science-related
Burt	Physics	33
Catherine	Psychology	33
Edward	Electronics	17
Ian	Chemistry, physics	50
Jack	–	0
George	Horticulture	100
Marc	–	0
Martin	PE	33
Mary	Biology, chemistry	57
Nicky	Human biology, sports science	67
Paul	–	0
Rebecca	–	0
Richard	–	0
Robert	Electronics	33
Sue	–	0

Reflections on Year 11

There are many ways of looking at these accounts over the five years of how pupil and parental hopes developed. In some cases (e.g. George) pupils were going on to do pretty well exactly what they had wanted to do for years. In other cases (e.g. Sue) circumstances had led them to have to reduce their aspirations. For most of the pupils, their hopes gradually focused over the five years, informed no doubt by feedback from their teachers as well as by other influences.

One notable feature was that of the 15 pupils still at Pasmoor School at the end of Year 11 out of the original 21 in the mixed-ability class with which I started at the beginning of Year 7, 14 (i.e. 93 per cent) were going on to full-time study rather than leaving to gain employment or for any other reason (e.g. to bring up children). In England, as in many industrialized countries, the percentage of school-leavers remaining in education has risen considerably over recent years (Centre for Educational Research and Innovation 1998) and, in addition, the school is in one of the wealthier parts of the UK, with employment rates and wages above the national average.

As a science educator I was interested in how many of the pupils were going on to make some direct use of their science in their education or work after they had left Pasmoor School. To a certain extent, this depends on one's definition of science (Reiss 1993b). Obviously studying horticulture at agricultural college involves studying science but what about psychology at A level? I would say this does too. What then about A level sociology or GNVQ built environment or boat-building? That's more difficult to say!

Table 6.3 lists for the 15 pupils still at Pasmoor School at the end of Year 11 any aspects of their further study that, in my opinion, include science. I have also, *very* tentatively, attempted to quantify the percentage of what each pupil was going on to study that was science-related. I have excluded from this definition such subjects as computing, geography, IT, mathematics, photography and sociology which, arguably, include aspects of science. In my view, therefore, the percentages included in Table 6.3 are, if anything, on the low side. Had technology-related subjects been included, the percentages would have been higher and fewer pupils would have scored 0 per cent.

Despite this rather 'narrow' definition of science, 9 of the 15 (i.e. 60 per cent) pupils were going to make direct use of the school science in their further study. I mention this because many UK science educators seem to assume that only a very small proportion of school-leavers go on to study science (references charitably omitted).

Despite its unpopularity at the end of Year 10 (see p. 123), two of the pupils (Ian and Mary) were going on to study chemistry/chemistry-related subjects (assuming horticulture and PE are not classified as chemistry-related). It has, though, to be said that this is fewer than the number going on to study physics/physics-related subjects (four: Burt, Edward, Ian and Robert) or biology/biology-related subjects (five: Catherine, George, Mary, Martin and Nicky). Indeed, Mary made it extremely clear in her Year 11 interview that it was only her career intentions that were making her take chemistry.

There was a significant but not a particularly strong relationship between how well pupils had done in their science GCSEs and whether or not they were going on to study science. (Calculating the Spearman rank correlation coefficient between the average number of GCSE science points for each pupil ($A^* = 8$, $A = 7$, $B = 6$, etc.) and the approximate percentage of what each pupil was going on to study that would be science-related gives $r_s = 0.51$; $0.05 < p < 0.10$; two-tailed; 5 per cent value $= 0.52$. This implies that 26 per cent of the variation in what each pupil was going on to study that would be science-related can be explained by variation in how well the pupils had done in their science GCSEs.)

I had begun my study hoping that it might shed light on two main questions:

• How do pupils experience school science lessons?
• Why do some pupils enjoy science and do well in it, while others don't?

The final chapter, Chapter 7, addresses these questions further.

Key points

- Year 11 was largely concerned with finishing the syllabus, revising and taking GCSEs.
- The pupils I was following did extremely well in their GCSE science exams.
- In some cases on leaving school pupils were going on to do what they had wanted to do for years. In other cases circumstances had led them to have to reduce their aspirations. For most of the pupils, their aims had gradually focused over the five years.
- Of the 15 pupils I had followed from the beginning of Year 7 through to the end of Year 11, 14 were continuing with full-time education and 9 were going on to make direct use of their school science in this.
- Five of the pupils were going on to study biology/biology-related subjects, four to study physics/physics-related subjects and two to study chemistry.
- There was a significant relationship, but not a particularly strong one, between how well pupils had done in their science GCSEs and whether or not they were going on to study science.

7

Children learning science?

Ms. Shapiro:	Can you tell me why the pencil appears bent in the water?
Yasmin:	No! [laughs]
Ms. Shapiro:	Do you think that it is important to know?
Yasmin:	Well, yes. Like if we have a test on it, then yes, we have to know it and study it and learn it.
Ms. Shapiro:	And if there is no test, do you think that it is important or valuable to know these things about light?
Yasmin:	No. I don't think so. They're sort of fun, but I don't think that it is something I am going to use ever.

(Shapiro 1994: 139)

How do pupils experience school science lessons?

One of the original aims of my study was to illustrate how pupils experience school science lessons. In large measure this is why I have spent a considerable amount of time describing a variety of lessons. My hope is that most of the pupils, teachers and learning support assistants involved in this study won't be too greatly surprised by these accounts on reading them! More generally, one of my intentions was to document for other people, including parents, teachers and researchers, the sorts of educational experiences presented to pupils by an above-average science department in an English secondary state school in the late 1990s.

In places I have chosen simply to cite what I heard or observed rather than explicitly passing comment on it. There are several reasons for this. For one thing, I am conscious that the author of a book is already in a most privileged position. After all, I have selected what to cite. Simply through the selectivity of such citation and the way such incidences are positioned I am passing judgement and, at least to some extent, even influencing how you may read such records. More extensive appraisal might be unfair. More mundanely, the book would be lengthened enormously if every incident and quotation was accompanied by a commentary. And then there is the fact that in biographies I generally prefer the recitation of anecdotes and presentation of history to too much interpretation by the biographer. In terms of genre, I prefer plays to books of literary criticism and films to interpretative documentaries.

One of the conclusions I reached during the study was that for the great majority of the pupils science education played a small part in their lives. Attempts by me on all six interviews I did with the pupils to get them to talk in any detail about what they had learnt in their science lessons were not especially successful. For example, the same pupils who were both happy and able to talk to me at their Year 11 interviews cogently and in some detail about their sex education classes, the extent of drug use at the school, the prevalence of bullying, differences between the ways that boys and girls behave and their favourite science teachers were often unable to give me what I would consider to be a reasonable answer to the question 'What's the most useful thing you reckon you learnt in science at Pasmoor School?'

Perhaps my favourite answer to this question was delivered in all seriousness by one of the six pupils who got AA or better in their science GCSEs. The pupil stated 'That's a hard one! Reflection and refraction really. 'Cos that really helps when you're playing snooker – you know how things rebound'.

Now, while this is just an anecdote, it illustrates a more important point which is that I don't believe existing science curricula ever require pupils to reflect on *why* they are learning in science what they are learning. To be bluntly honest, there were times when I wondered why on earth pupils were studying the science they were. In particular, there seemed to be a time in Year 11 when lesson after lesson in chemistry consisted of relative molecular masses. I admit I was the sort of pupil who genuinely derived considerable intellectual satisfaction from understanding relative molecular masses. But I can't claim that for the overwhelming majority of people they are either relevant or intelligible. Of course, the chemistry teachers at Pasmoor School spent so long on this topic – as I would have done had I been teaching chemistry at the school – because answering such topics well in exams enables pupils to achieve higher grades. And Pasmoor science department did an extremely good job at getting pupils to do well at science GCSE – as the data in Chapter 6 make clear.

Many other authors have raised questions about the relevance of school science for those pupils who don't go on to study science subsequently. For example, Jarman and McAleese (1996) found that when they asked 15-year-old pupils in Northern Ireland 'Can you tell me about an occasion when you used the science you learnt in school in your own everyday life?', a number of pupils found the question quite surprising, almost perplexing. The most common answer was to do with wiring plugs.

To a science educator it is somewhat disheartening to think that the principal fruit of 11 years of mandatory science lessons is that pupils believe they have helped them to wire a plug. That science is important because it can show you how to wire a plug was also an argument made by Year 11 pupils in Osborne and Collins' (1999) study. This study found, as I did, that the majority of the negative comments about school science concerned chemistry.

Perhaps I can mention what I consider to be a significant illustration of how some science educators have misunderstood the notion of relevance by citing from a study undertaken in the pseudonymous 'Owens County', a rural county in the USA. The author, writing in perhaps the most prestigious science education journal there is, states:

> Owens County teachers made a conscious effort to relate science to the everyday lives of students. For example, during one lesson the fifth-grade teacher illustrated principles of motion through a kickball demonstration. A third-grade instructor had students conjecture about how simple acts like obtaining water would be different if performed on the moon rather than in Owens County.
>
> (Charron 1991: 683)

Now, I am very much in favour of third-graders being encouraged to think about how living on the Moon would compare to living on Earth. But the argument in favour of such teaching is not that it is relevant (as that word is normally understood) but that when it is done well it stretches the mind, fascinates, intrigues and provides new insights into the workings of the physical universe. I am confident that even a richly developed understanding of how to obtain water on the Moon will be of little practical relevance to most of the future citizens of Owens County.

Why do some pupils enjoy science and do well in it, while others don't?

It is widely recognized in the UK and in a number of other countries that pupils enter their secondary schooling (around the age of 11 years) with high expectations of science and a positive attitude towards it. Over the succeeding years, though, interest in science generally wanes, especially in chemistry and physics (see Osborne *et al.* 1998; Parkinson *et al.* 1998; Ramsden 1998; Lindahl 1999), though this is a feature across subjects in general rather than specific to science (Sutcliffe 1998).

What I would like to do here is to look at the various factors that I believe are important in determining whether pupils in general, and those at Pasmoor School I was following in particular, enjoy science and do well in it or not. I shall look, in no especial order at:

- the importance of the school;
- the importance of the curriculum;
- the importance of teachers;
- the importance of the home;
- the importance of peers;
- the importance of the pupil her- or himself.

The importance of the school

By most accounts, Pasmoor School was a 'good school'. It had two Ofsted (Office for Standards in Education) inspections during the five years I was visiting and both were extremely complimentary, the second one especially so with regard to the science department. While many of the parents voiced specific criticisms of the school (e.g. with regard to setting, communications with the school and revision), only one parent of the 15 pupils still at Pasmoor School at the end of Year 11 wished their child had not gone there. Most of the parents were pleased with what the school had done for their children and a few spoke about the school extremely positively.

There was, though, as the following quotes from the Year 11 parental interviews indicate, a considerable degree of agreement among parents that Pasmoor School was best for the more able pupils:

> It does sometimes seem like they're only interested in manipulating the figures [percentage of GCSE passes at grades A* to C].
>
> (George's father)

> If you study . . . but otherwise they can't be bothered.
>
> (George's mother)

> I feel the ones who are really brainy they get really good support . . . middle of the road, like Martin, you find there's no encouragement.
>
> (Martin's mother)

> We haven't had any problems. If she hadn't been an able pupil, I think our views would be less [positive].
>
> (Nicky's mother)

> Basically they're not interested in Foundation . . . the As and A*s they can't do enough for.
>
> (Paul's mother)

When, in Years 7, 8 and 9, I asked those members of the science department who had been there for at least a few years how the school had changed I received a fairly consistent set of answers. Staff spoke positively about how the science department had developed (each quote comes from a different teacher but, for rather obvious reasons, I decided not to attribute quotes to teachers in this section):

> It was quite a fragmented department . . . a lot of disillusionment. Roland's worked extremely hard and there has been a lot of change of staff. Now it's one of the strongest departments in the school. Has a much higher profile . . . We do academically well by all the children.

> Department-wise it's improved immensely – much more organized; much more enthusiastic.

However, some in the science department talked with regret about how the ethos of the school had changed (again, each quote comes from a different teacher and quotes are unattributed):

> Maybe the ethos had changed a little bit. On a personal level I don't agree with that at all . . . though I understand why it was undertaken . . . exam-results driven.

> It's got much more, umm, management-oriented, rather than pupil-oriented, I feel. On the surface it's much more organized. I'm not convinced it is underneath.

> Much more a business now than a school . . . I think it's a little bit sad.

> Ethos has changed dramatically . . . and the underlying philosophy . . . When I came here it was very much a community school . . . People expected schools to deal with social issues . . . Now schools [are] more focused in terms of education . . . education seen in a different way . . . to deliver a curriculum . . . National Curriculum has had a lot to do with this . . . we've become much more expert in a much smaller area.

On the other hand, one member of the science department, while describing the changes in much the same terms as the preceding quote, welcomed them:

> The whole tone and focus of the school has shifted . . . a lot more focus on the standard of pupil achievement . . . role of the tutor moving very much . . . how can I put it? . . . less of a social worker and more towards guidance and monitoring pupil progress . . . ethos of the school committed to the pupils . . . makes the job more enjoyable, less of a policeman, more of maximizing learning and seeing progress.

I suspect that many teachers in English and Welsh schools over the last decade would talk similarly about the consequences of the educational reforms of the late 1980s and early 1990s for school ethos and for the priorities of schools.

One particular feature of schooling which the study caused me to reflect on more than I had previously was the provision made in mainstream schools for children with certain special needs. From Year 7, the parents of Burt, Edward and Rodney had all expressed concern about their sons' dyslexia. Whatever the strengths of Pasmoor's learning support assistants it was clear that they had never been trained more than superficially to provide the specific targeted help that could especially benefit such pupils. Nationally it is acknowledged that training for learning support assistants is patchy while too many of them have low salaries and temporary contracts (Farrell *et al.* 1999).

I admit that I too knew rather little about dyslexia at the start of this study. However, realizing the very considerable significance it had for Burt, Edward and Rodney caused me to read widely (e.g. Townend 1994; Silver 1998; Miles and Miles 1999), to contact The Dyslexia Institute and to begin to notice in the educational literature and on web sites references to conferences on dyslexia and to new theories about its causation and treatment. I also found myself reading up about other conditions such as dyspraxia and attention deficit (hyperactivity) disorder. This is not the place to launch into a review of what I learnt. Suffice it to note here that most schools – and I am sure Pasmoor School is no different from the great majority of schools in this respect – have probably never had the time and resources to ensure that they do the best for all their pupils.

A final point in this section is to consider what types of school are more likely subsequently to have pupils go on and study science. This area remains under-researched and some studies have failed to come up with any clear-cut conclusions (e.g. Sharp *et al.* 1996). One finding is that the provision of extracurricular activities in science which stimulate the imagination and creativity of pupils can be important (Woolnough 1994). Pasmoor School had an Ecology Club and participated with success in a number of local and national competitions which rewarded out-of-school activities.

The importance of the curriculum

The English and Welsh National Curriculum has been extensively critiqued since its introduction for its content and assessment arrangements and for the consequences these have had for classroom practice (e.g. in science, see Hacker and Rowe 1997; Donnelly and Jenkins 1999). I have already referred more than once to the influence that both the Year 9 SATs and the Years 10–11 GCSEs had on the science teaching at Pasmoor School.

It is widely acknowledged that pupils in England and Wales spend more time on exams than do pupils in any other country in Europe. Perhaps as a result, the biggest single worry for 8–15-year-olds in England and Wales in 1996, according to a major survey, was 'Failing tests or exams' with 44 per cent of the sample saying they 'often' worried about this (Ghate and Daniels 1997). In Ghate and Daniels' study, children were presented with a list of 11 things and asked whether they worried about them often, sometimes, hardly ever or never. The next thing after 'Failing tests or exams' that children most worried about was 'Someone in the family getting ill' (36 per cent). In the week in which I write this there is a report in the *TES* that 'Ministers intend to launch two more exams, for able nine and 13-year-olds' (Cassidy 1999).

Pasmoor School science department strongly recommended that pupils purchase a set of three revision guides for their GCSE science examinations – Parsons (n.d.a, n.d.b, n.d.c) for foundation level, or Parsons (n.d.d, n.d.e, n.d.f) for higher level. Each of these six books has a two-paragraph introduction, the second one of which is worth quoting and speaks for itself:

> Throughout these books there is constant emphasis on the inescapable need to ***keep learning the basic facts***. This simple message is hammered

home without compromise and without remorse; and while this traditionally brutal philosophy may not be quite in line with some other approaches to education, we still rather like it. But only because it works.

(Parsons n.d.: title page)

As the GCSEs approached, the number of hours' homework and revision that some pupils did became very considerable. At the same time (April of Year 11), national newspapers reported that revision guides and practice exam papers were outselling popular fiction. Many of the pupils put in two or more hours a night and said that they 'hated it', that they 'cancelled quite a lot of after-school activities' or that their 'social life went down the drain'. One pupil told me that she was doing '20, 25 hours a week' of homework and revision throughout Year 11.

When one takes into account the fact that several of the pupils had part-time jobs, the total weekly amount of time spent on school, homework, revision and paid employment for some pupils must have exceeded the upper limit of 48 hours currently stipulated in the European Union Working Hours Directive. Perhaps understandably, the pupil who spent 20 to 25 hours a week on homework and revision talked with considerable insight about international comparisons of the amount of time pupils spent on homework, something she had read about in *The Times*.

Turning from assessment to classroom practice, the introduction in 1989 of mandatory 'investigations' across the 5–16 science curriculum, while broadly welcomed, has been criticized for presenting too narrow a view of what science is and for being unrealistic for teachers to implement (Jenkins 1995; Donnelly *et al.* 1996). Certainly at Pasmoor School my own experience was that investigations, particularly in the GCSE years, became not what I would consider to be true, open-ended investigations but routines in which the teachers did their very best to ensure that pupils repeated parts of investigations sufficiently often to allow them to score as high a set of marks as possible.

A national survey carried out in 1998 showed that most pupils at the end of their GCSE science course see the main functions of scientific investigations as 'getting a good mark ... Many felt that school investigations bore little relationship to what it was like to work as a scientist' (Nott and Wellington 1999: 1).

The question of the functions of school science education has been widely debated in recent years. Increasingly, it has been agreed that school science education should serve the needs of the whole school population (Millar 1996). For this reason, scientific literacy, however this term is understood, is seen as the prime aim of science teaching (see also Layton *et al.* 1993; Irwin and Wynne 1996; Hodson 1998). Generally, scientific literacy is seen as being a vehicle to help tomorrow's adults to understand scientific issues (Gräber and Bolte 1997). In the UK, for example, it might be hoped that a good school science curriculum would help us to understand the uncertainties around genetically modified foods, global warming or the radiation from mobile phones.

I am fully in agreement with this understanding of scientific literacy, so far as it goes. More recent work has argued that science education should advance democracy (Longbottom 1999), enable pupils to grow as persons (Reiss 1999) or better the world (Roth and Lee in preparation). Indeed, the notion of scientific literacy can be taken further by considering the three axes of 'the here and now', 'space' and 'resistance' (Reiss in press).

For a start, we should not only think of school science education providing skills and information for the citizens of tomorrow; it should be absolutely relevant to the pupils being taught today, i.e. in *the here and now*. Obvious examples of topics pertinent to pupils that could be meaningfully taught in school science include ones presently covered (though often in only a rather cursory fashion) in health education and environmental education within science.

For example, the issue of cigarette smoking is typically, in my experience, covered in school science lessons by means of a practical demonstration that cigarettes contain tar, backed up by a series of polemics (often reinforced through the making of posters by pupils) that smoking is bad for you. Certainly this was the case at Pasmoor School (see p. 52). More time in science curricula would allow for both a more detailed and a more nuanced treatment. For instance, pupils could be taught more about the addictive nature of nicotine, about possible health benefits of smoking (there is some evidence for a negative relationship between the risk of developing Alzheimer's disease and the number of cigarettes smoked) and about the reasons why people take up smoking.

Pupils could also, in science lessons, PSHE (personal, social and health education) lessons or citizenship lessons, consider whether the aim of education about smoking should be one of beneficence (doing good, e.g. by persuading pupils not to smoke) or one of the promotion of autonomy (i.e. enabling pupils to make their own rational, informed choices) – see Reiss (1996). It would also be worth seeing whether pupils' writings could have audiences beyond their teacher and peers. For example, instead of constructing posters about smoking, destined never to leave the confines of school lab walls, pupils could produce desktop-published leaflets for distribution in GP surgeries or, failing that, at least in the school visitor area. This would help writing in science lessons to be more authentic.

A second way in which the notion that school science education ought to be for the benefit of the whole school population can be taken further is by accepting the idea that education can help provide pupils with *space* in which to live their lives. This idea has its roots in the work of Solomon (1992) who looked at how pupils learn about energy. She found that pupils do not simply learn a single meaning for the term 'energy'. Instead, they get to know about its several meanings in a variety of ways. Indeed, pupils are perfectly capable of holding a number of alternative understandings (or 'mental models') simultaneously.

From such work it can be argued that the job of school science lessons about energy is not to provide pupils with only a single model of energy. Rather, we should aim to provide pupils with a variety of models that can be used appropriately in different contexts. Pupils should be helped to develop a number of intellectual 'spaces' which they can inhabit as occasion requires. We all know the stereotype of the scientist who can only see a rainbow in terms of the reflection and refraction of light. Such a knowledge is incomplete. A fuller understanding of rainbows in the culture I inhabit comes from seeing Constable's water-colours, reading the poems of Wordsworth and knowing about the story of Noah's flood.

Finally, science education has the potential to serve as a platform for *resistance*, a notion just beginning to be explored in some science education writing (see Rodriguez 1998), though well established in anti-racist education circles (e.g. Ahmed *et al.* 1998). For example, in a paper about teaching science to homeless children in an urban setting in the USA, Barton writes about 13-year-old Gilma. Gilma took the lead in a project, developed by the children themselves, to study pollution in their local community. Barton concluded that the main reason for Gilma's enthusiastic participation in this project in her community was 'to figure out how to make it better for herself, her friends, and her family' (Barton 1998: 385).

The importance of teachers

Teachers, as governments frequently remind the electorate while giving them pay rises below the average, are of crucial importance in education. However, the multifaceted nature of what it takes to be a good teacher has made it difficult for researchers to come up with more than fairly obvious conclusions about what it is that makes a really good teacher (e.g. Sammons *et al.* 1997).

I am convinced that much of the teaching provided by members of the science department at Pasmoor School was of exceptionally high quality. I have already reviewed in Chapter 5, the views of Year 10 pupils as to what constitutes a good teacher and I hope that the descriptions of the lessons I have provided indicate the range of teaching approaches adopted by the various science teachers in the school.

On the Year 11 interviews I asked the pupils to tell me who their favourite teacher was and to explain why. Their explanations don't add a great deal to those given in Year 10 (see p. 124) in answer to the question 'Tell me about the sort of science teaching you like' because the Year 11 question was generally answered by pupils as they had answered the Year 10 one. I was interested, though, to note that the 16 pupils (i.e. the 15 still at Pasmoor School plus Rodney) gave a total of 27 names belonging to nine different teachers. In other words, there was no one universally favourite teacher, though one teacher was nominated eight times and another six times.

Several pupils nominated teachers who hadn't taught them in the last two years and one boy nominated someone who hadn't taught him for three years. The five girls nominated a total of 10 female teachers' names and no male teachers' names. The eleven boys nominated a total of 12 female teachers' names and 5 male teachers' names. While the numbers are too small to draw firm conclusions, this raises the possibility that boys may be more likely than girls to nominate male teachers as their favourites in much the same way that male teachers were more likely than female teachers to talk about male pupils when I asked them about the pupils in their classes (see p. 91).

The importance of the home

There is a considerable literature on the importance of the home environment for educational success. Various statistical analyses in England and in other countries have shown the negative effect on GCSE and other examination scores (both in science and in other subjects) of such factors as being entitled to free school meals, coming from a home without a car, coming from a home with no adult in employment and having a father in socioeconomic Classes 4 or 5 (Croxford 1997; Gibson and Asthana 1998; Hackett 1999; Strand 1999).

Similarly, the National Child Development Study, which has followed a group of 17,000 people born in Britain in one week in 1958, has shown that at the age of 37 years, numeracy and literacy are significantly correlated to such additional factors as whether the participants' parents had been in education post-16 and whether participants recalled there being more than 25 books in their childhood home (Parsons and Bynner 1998).

Unsurprisingly, these factors mean that there is a strong correlation between social class and the chances of going on to higher education (Robinson and White 1997; Edwards *et al.* 1998).

The advantage of such large-scale correlation-type studies is that they hammer home the importance of social class and related factors. But, of course, there are more subtle reasons why the home is important. For a start, back in 1967 the Plowden Committee concluded that it was not material home circumstances but parental attitudes which explained more of the variance in pupil achievement (Department of Education and Science 1967). Then, as a result of a study about how parents of primary pupils used materials with which they had been provided for use at home to work with their children on simple science investigations, it has been argued that the richness of the variety of home cultures not only cannot be reduced to numbers but almost defies categorization (Solomon 1994).

One of the significant ways in which the home backgrounds of a number of the pupils followed here changed during the five years of the study was when their parents split up. This happened to six of the pupils – Jack, Liz, Marc, Michael, Peter and Sue. (I have no data for Jane's parents after Year 7 or for Clive's parents after Year 8.) I absolutely do not wish to make facile or simplistic suggestions about any connections between one's parents splitting up and one not doing well at school. Nevertheless, there is strong evidence that children whose parents separate tend to perform less well in school and to gain fewer educational qualifications. Indeed, the death of a parent does not carry the same risks to a child of poorer educational attainment and poorer mental health as does coming from a home where parents split up (Rodgers and Pryor 1998).

One can imagine that children can react to parental separation in a number of ways. In some cases, a child may even end up doing better educationally than would otherwise have been the case, for instance if they take refuge in their studies. However, it is hardly surprising that it is more usual for the break-up of a relationship between a pupil's parents to have a negative effect on that pupil's educational achievements. One can propose several reasons for this. For example, parents who are splitting up may, very understandably, be preoccupied with other matters and less able to provide the stability that helps in such mundane matters as regular assistance with homework. More importantly, perhaps, while the ending of an unhealthy relationship can sometimes be to the benefit of children, many children find parental break-up deeply unsettling even if they are unable at the time, or even subsequently, to articulate this.

Another way in which the home can be important is indicated by an international study which showed that in a number of countries pupils intending to study science at university level were more likely to have had one or more parents with a scientific degree (Woolnough *et al.* 1995). However, the actual values of the correlation coefficients for such studies are low; in other words, there is a lot of scatter.

Thinking of the 15 pupils in this study, there was some evidence for a connection between pupils going on to study science as 16–19-year-olds and parental scientific education, as can be seen by comparing the parental biographies in Chapter 3 with Table 6.3 – for example, for George, Ian and Nicky. At the same time, though, there are the exceptions, such as Mary.

The importance of peers

For too long psychologists have simply argued about whether heredity *or* the environment are more important in the determination of personality and behaviour. More recent studies have looked at the way in which both heredity *and* environment are important. One important aspect of a pupil's environment is their peers. Indeed, some psychologists have begun to argue that peer environment may be more important than home environment in certain respects. It is noteworthy that bullying by one's peers is associated with poorer physical and mental health in various countries (Forero *et al.* 1999; Kaltiala-Heino *et al.* 1999).

One of the most obvious manifestations of peer culture is its differentiation by gender. In earlier chapters I have referred in some detail to various differences between how girls and boys behaved and were treated. My own understanding is that throughout our lives there are strong societal pressures on us to differentiate ourselves by sex. During childhood this means that girls will (often) be girls and boys will (often) be boys. Of course, there are many exceptions to this: girls and boys are not homogenous groups (e.g. Mac an Ghaill 1994). However, pressures both from peers and from society more generally push pupils towards stereotyped sex-specific behaviours.

So boys are more likely to be noisy and aggressive and girls quiet and passive (Urquhart 1996). Equally, girls are more likely to prefer biology and boys physics (Solomon 1997; Vlaeminke *et al.* 1997), while the sexes often come to see science differently (Levine and Geldman-Caspar 1996; Jovanovic and King 1998).

In common with many schools, Pasmoor School put a lot of effort into trying to combat such gender-stereotypical behaviour though, so far as I was aware, it did nothing explicitly to try to reduce the fairly widespread incidence of homophobic taunts, which I heard directed at boys by boys from Year 7 upwards.

Until around the early 1990s, gender issues in schools in England were generally to do with raising the educational attainment of girls. Since then, it has increasingly been realized that it is more likely to be boys than girls who are underachieving. As Pasmoor School's *Annual Report to Parents 1997–1998* put it:

> Boys are still under performing when matched against the girls. They continue to reflect the national trend achieving successes in the higher grades, 10 per cent below those of the girls. We have focused on this issue throughout the last two years, both in discussion groups amongst the school staff and in the classroom, particularly in the Year 9 single sex classes in English. The experiences of the English staff and the comments of parents have led us to conclude that the latter experience has boosted the confidence of boys in the communication skills.

When I asked pupils at the Year 11 interviews how they would compare the behaviour of girls and boys in lessons, many of them were happy to make generalizations but added that there were exceptions to these:

> The boys talk; we get told off. The girls talk and the teachers join in about *EastEnders* . . . They're perceived as doing more work even if they aren't. They're more tactful.
>
> (Burt)

> Umm. I think the boys are a lot more, like chatty and noisy. And I think they're slow workers as well. But then the girls are like chatty as well, but they're quieter about it.
>
> (Catherine)

> Right, well, saying that boys are more boisterous is, sorry to say it, bullshit. The girls are very outspoken and they get away with it more . . . Boys do take it much less seriously . . . boys . . . finish off homework just before lesson.
>
> (Edward)

Girls behave; boys don't. That's basically what it's like . . . there are a few girls who cause havoc and a few boys who don't . . . the girls tend to get away with more.

(George)

On the whole I'd say girls are better behaved, more mature, don't mess around so much but there are groups of girls who can . . . misbehave . . . but they don't . . . throw things about.

(Jack)

I think the girls towards the end of the five years were more concentrated. More into the work than the lads were. I dunno why.

(Marc)

Girls, I think personally, are a lot more focused on what they're doing. Boys take a more laid back attitude.

(Martin)

I'd say that it depends what type of boy they are, 'cos if they're really studying they'll behave . . . overall girls behave better. I don't know why. I think boys have something to prove in their own minds.

(Rebecca)

Umm. I'd say girls are more responsible. I guess everyone says that. Some boys don't really care; most of the girls get on with it.

(Richard)

The importance of the pupil her- or himself

The school, the curriculum, one's teachers, one's home and one's peers are all important for educational achievement and for how a pupil experiences their schooling. Ultimately, though, for any pupil, enjoyment and success at school in general and in science in particular can only partly be explained by such external factors.

One study that looked at the significance of family, peers and school cultures for whether or not pupils engaged with their schoolwork usefully emphasized the notion of boundaries (Phelan *et al.* 1991). The idea here is that as pupils move from one context to another (e.g. from home to school) they cross boundaries. When the world of school and the world of home are congruent, there are smooth transitions across such boundaries. When school and home belong to different worlds, crossings are impossible. In like vein, Glen Aikenhead has written about the extent to which science education expects school pupils to acquire the distinct subculture of science (Aikenhead 1996; Aikenhead and Jegede 1999).

One of my main conclusions is that school science education can only succeed when pupils believe that the science they are being taught is of personal worth to themselves. Here, 'personal worth' should not be construed too narrowly. For many pupils, science is of value only in so far as it is of instrumental use, for example for further education. Other pupils, though, search for meanings and may feel that science can help them to understand their place in the world. Such diversity among pupils means that a science curriculum and a way of teaching science cannot assume that there is only one reason for learning about science. But unless science teaching genuinely engages with the concerns of real pupils, they will be more than capable of learning little from it.

Key points

- For most of the pupils in the study, science education played a small part in their lives.
- Examination success played an important part in the life of Pasmoor School. The pseudonym I chose for the school was an appropriate one.
- Science curricula could be reformed so as to be of more value to pupils.
- Much of the teaching provided by members of the science department at Pasmoor School was of exceptionally high quality.
- Pupils' home backgrounds are important for their educational success.
- Peers affect how school is experienced by pupils.
- School science education can only succeed when pupils believe that the science they are being taught is of personal worth to themselves.

References

Ahmed, J., Gulam, W.A. and Hapeshi, D. (1998) Brickbats, survival and resistance. *Multicultural Teaching*, 16(3): 7–14.

Aikenhead, G.S. (1996) Science education: border crossing into the subculture of science. *Studies in Science Education*, 27: 1–52.

Aikenhead, G.S. and Jegede, O.J. (1999) Cross-cultural science education: a cognitive explanation of a cultural phenomenon. *Journal of Research in Science Teaching*, 36: 269–87.

Aristotle ([n.d.]1976) *The Nicomachean Ethics*, translated by J.A.K. Thomson, revised by H. Tredennick. London: Penguin.

Astor, R.A., Meyer, H.A. and Behre, W.J. (1999) Unowned places and times: maps and interviews about violence in high schools. *American Educational Research Journal*, 36: 3–42.

Barton, A.C. (1998) Teaching science with homeless children: pedagogy, representation, and identity. *Journal of Research in Science Teaching*, 35: 379–94.

Benton, P. (1995) Recipe fictions . . . literary fast food? Reading interests in Year 8. *Oxford Review of Education*, 21: 99–111.

Black, P. (1995) 1987 to 1995 – the struggle to formulate a National Curriculum for science in England and Wales. *Studies in Science Education*, 26: 159–88.

Black, P. and Atkin, J.M. (eds) (1996) *Changing the Subject: Innovation in Science, Mathematics and Technology*. London: Routledge.

Bleach, K., Blagden, T., Ebbutt, D. *et al.* (1996) *What Difference Does it Make? An Investigation of Factors Influencing the Motivation and Performance of Year 8 Boys in a West Midlands Comprehensive School*. Wolverhampton: Educational Research Unit, University of Wolverhampton School of Education.

Campbell, B. (1999) Classroom continuity: pupils' perceptions of science education at primary and secondary school. *Proceedings of the Second International Conference of the European Science Education Research Association*: 587–9.

Casement, P. (1985) *On Learning from the Patient*. London: Tavistock.

Cassidy, S. (1999) Labour heralds birth of super test, *TES*, 17 September: 1.

Centre for Educational Research and Innovation (1998) *Education at a Glance: OECD Indicators 1998*. Paris: Organisation for Economic Co-operation and Development.

Charron, E.H. (1991) Classroom and community influences on youths' perceptions of science in a rural county school system. *Journal of Research in Science Teaching*, 28: 671–87.

Cohen, L. and Manion, L. (1994) *Research Methods in Education*, 4th edn. London: Routledge.

Croxford, L. (1997) Participation in science subjects: the effect of the Scottish curriculum framework. *Research Papers in Education*, 12: 69–89.

Davies, W.D. (1967) *Invitation to the New Testament: A Guide to its Main Witnesses*. London: Darton, Longman & Todd.

Delamont, S., Benyon, J. and Atkinson, P. (1988) In the beginning was the Bunsen: the foundations of secondary school science. *Qualitative Studies in Education*, 1: 315–28.

Department of Education and Science (1967) *Children and their Primary Schools: A Report of the Central Advisory Council for Education (England)*. London: HMSO.

Department of Education and Science and the Welsh Office (1991) *Science in the National Curriculum (1991)*. London: HMSO.

Donnelly, J.F. and Jenkins, E.W. (1999) *Science Teaching in Secondary Schools under the National Curriculum*. Leeds: University of Leeds Centre for Studies in Science and Mathematics Education & University of Leeds Centre for Policy Studies in Education.

Donnelly, J., Buchan, A., Jenkins, E., Laws, P. and Welford, G. (1996) *Investigations by Order: Policy, Curriculum and Science Teachers' Work under the Education Reform Act*. Nafferton: Studies in Education.

Edwards, T., Power, S., Whitty, G. and Wigfall, V. (1998) Destined for success? Academic ability and career trajectories. Conference paper, British Educational Research Association, Belfast, 27–30 August.

Equal Opportunities Commission and OFSTED (1996) *The Gender Divide: Performance Differences between Boys and Girls at School*. London: HMSO.

Farrell, P., Polat, F. and Balshaw, M. (1999) *The Management, Role and Training of Learning Support Assistants*. London: Department for Education and Employment.

Forero, R., McLellan, L., Rissel, C. and Bauman, A. (1999) Bullying behaviour and psychosocial health among school students in New South Wales, Australia: cross sectional survey. *British Medical Journal*, 319: 344–8.

Ghate, D. and Daniels, A. (1997) *Talking About My Generation: A Survey of 8–15 Year Olds Growing Up in the 1990s*. London: National Society for the Prevention of Cruelty to Children.

Gibson, A. and Asthana, S. (1998) Schools, pupils and examination results: contextualising school 'performance'. *British Educational Research Journal*, 24: 269–82.

Goodall, J. (1986) *The Chimpanzees of Gombe: Patterns of Behavior*. Cambridge, MA: Belknap Press of Harvard University Press.

Gräber, W. and Bolte, C. (eds) (1997) *Scientific Literacy: An International Symposium IPN 154*. Kiel: Institut für die Pädagogik der Naturwissenschaften an der Universitatät Kiel.

Hacker, R.G. and Rowe, M.J. (1997) The impact of a National Curriculum development on teaching and learning behaviours. *International Journal of Science Education*, 19: 997–1004.

Hackett, G. (1999) Flagship council flagging, *TES*, 29 January: 6.

Harding, J. (1992) *Breaking the Barrier: Girls in Science Education*. Paris: International Institute for Educational Planning (established by UNESCO).

Hawkey, R. (1995) Primary children's expectations of secondary school science. *Primary Science Review*, 39: 16–7.

Hayes, J.H. and Holladay, C.R. (1982) *Biblical Exegesis: A Beginner's Handbook*. Atlanta, GA: John Knox.

Helldén, G. (1998a) A longitudinal study of students' conceptualization of ecological processes. Conference paper, Annual Meeting of the National Association for Research in Science Teaching, San Diego, 19–22 April.

Helldén, G. (1998b) A longitudinal study of pupils' conceptualisation of the role of the flower. Conference paper, Second Conference of European Researchers in Didaktik of Biology, Göteborg, 18–22 November.

Helldén, G. (1999) Personal context and continuity of human thought; recurrent themes in a longitudinal study of pupils' understanding of scientific phenomena. Conference paper, Second International Conference of the European Science Education Research Association, Kiel, 31 August–4 September.

Herbert, C.M.H. (1989) *Talking of Silence: The Sexual Harassment of Schoolgirls*. London: Falmer Press.

Hodson, D. (1998) *Teaching and Learning Science: Towards a Personalized Approach*. Buckingham: Open University Press.

Irwin, A. and Wynne, B. (eds) (1996) *Misunderstanding Science? The Public Reconstruction of Science and Technology*. Cambridge: Cambridge University Press.

Jarman, D. (1988) Interview heard on English television on 16 July 1994 where Derek Jarman was refusing to 'explain' his film *The Last of England*. 'They' refers to 'The viewers'.

Jarman, R. (1993) Real experiments with bunsen burners: pupils' perceptions of the similarities and differences between primary science and secondary science. *School Science Review*, 74(268): 19–29.

Jarman, R. and McAleese, L. (1996) A survey of children's reported use of school science in their everyday lives. *Research in Education*, 55: 1–16.

Jenkins, E.W. (1995) Central policy and teacher response? Scientific investigation in the national curriculum in England and Wales. *International Journal of Science Education*, 17: 471–80.

Jovanovic, J. and King, S.S. (1998) Boys and girls in the performance-based science classroom: who's doing the performing? *American Educational Research Journal*, 35: 477–96.

Joyner, R. (1995) *A Revision Guide for the National Curriculum Key Stage 3, Science (to Level 8)*. Hingham: Walrus Books.

Joyner, R. (1996) *A Revision Guide for the National Curriculum Key Stage 3, Levels 1 to 6 (post-Dearing)*. Hingham: Walrus Books.

Kaltiala-Heino, R., Rimpelä, M., Marttunen, M., Rimpelä, A. and Rantanen, P. (1999) Bullying, depression, and suicidal ideation in Finnish adolescents: school survey. *British Medical Journal*, 319: 348–51.

Kehily, M.J. and Nayak, A. (1997) Lads and laughter: humour and the production of heterosexual hierarchies. *Gender and Education*, 9: 69–87.

Layton, D., Jenkins, E., Macgill, S. and Davey, A. (1993) *Inarticulate Science? Perspectives on the Public Understanding of Science and Some Implications for Science Education*. Driffield: Studies in Education.

Lea, M. and West, L. (1995) Motives, mature students, the self and narrative, in J. Swindells (ed.) *The Uses of Autobiography*. London: Taylor & Francis.

Levine, T. and Geldman-Caspar, Z. (1996) Informal science writing produced by boys and girls: writing preference and quality. *British Educational Research Journal*, 22: 421–39.

Lindahl, B. (1999) How does schoolwork contribute to pupils' understanding and attitudes to science? What do 13-year-old pupils say about science? Conference paper, Second International Conference of the European Science Education Research Association, Kiel, 31 August–4 September.

Longbottom, J. (1999) Reconceptualising science education. Conference paper, Second International Conference of the European Science Education Research Association, Kiel, 31 August–4 September.

Mac an Ghaill, M. (1994) *The Making of Men: Masculinities, Sexualities and Schooling*. Buckingham: Open University Press.

MacBeath, J., Boyd, B., Rand J. and Bell, S. (1996) *Schools Speak for Themselves: Towards a Framework for Self-Evaluation*. London: National Union of Teachers.

Mayoh, K. and Knutton, S. (1997) Using out-of-school experience in science lessons: reality or rhetoric? *International Journal of Science Education*, 19: 849–67.

Miles, T.R. and Miles, E. (1999) *Dyslexia: A Hundred Years On*, 2nd edn. Buckingham: Open University Press.

Millar, R. (1996) Towards a science curriculum for public understanding. *School Science Review*, 77(280): 7–18.

Millar, R. and Osborne, J. (eds) (1998) *Beyond 2000: Science Education for the Future*. London: Nuffield Foundation.

Nott, M. and Wellington, J. (1999) High school students' views of scientific investigations. Conference paper, Second International Conference of the European Science Education Research Association, Kiel, 31 August–4 September.

Ogborn, J., Kress, G., Martins, I. and McGillicuddy, K. (1996) *Explaining Science in the Classroom*. Buckingham: Open University Press.

Osborne, J. and Collins, S. (1999) Pupils' and parents' views of the role and value of the science curriculum. Conference paper, British Educational Research Association, Brighton, September.

Osborne, J. and Simon, S. (1996) Primary science: past and future directions. *Studies in Science Education*, 26: 99–147.

Osborne, J., Driver, R. and Simon, S. (1998) Attitudes to science: issues and concerns. *School Science Review*, 79(288): 27–33.

Parkinson, J., Hendley, D., Tanner, H. and Stables, A. (1998) Pupils' attitudes to science in Key Stage 3 of the National Curriculum: a study of pupils in South Wales. *Research in Science & Technological Education*, 16: 165–76.

Parsons, R. (ed.) (n.d.a) *Revision Guide for GCSE Double Science Biology: Foundation Level for the New Syllabuses from 1998 Onwards*. Kirkby-in-Furness: The Science Coordination Group.

Parsons, R. (ed.) (n.d.b) *Revision Guide for GCSE Double Science Chemistry: Foundation Level for the New Syllabuses from 1998 Onwards*. Kirkby-in-Furness: The Science Coordination Group.

Parsons, R. (ed.) (n.d.c) *Revision Guide for GCSE Double Science Physics: Foundation Level for the New Syllabuses from 1998 Onwards*. Kirkby-in-Furness: The Science Coordination Group.

Parsons, R. (ed.) (n.d.d) *Revision Guide for GCSE Double Science Biology: Higher Level for the New Syllabuses from 1998 Onwards*. Kirkby-in-Furness: The Science Coordination Group.

Parsons, R. (ed.) (n.d.e) *Revision Guide for GCSE Double Science Chemistry: Higher Level for the New Syllabuses from 1998 Onwards.* Kirkby-in-Furness: The Science Coordination Group.

Parsons, R. (ed.) (n.d.f) *Revision Guide for GCSE Double Science Physics: Higher Level for the New Syllabuses from 1998 Onwards.* Kirkby-in-Furness: The Science Coordination Group.

Parsons, S. and Bynner, J. (1998) *Influences on Adult Basic Skills: Factors Affecting the Development of Literacy and Numeracy from Birth to 37.* London: The Basic Skills Agency.

Phelan, P., Davidson, A.L. and Cao, H.T. (1991) Students' multiple worlds: negotiating the boundaries of family, peer, and school cultures. *Anthropology & Education Quarterly*, 22: 224–50.

Plowman, L. (1999) *Using Video for Observing Interaction in the Classroom,* Spotlight 72. Edinburgh: Scottish Council for Research in Education.

Proust, M. ([1913]1943) *Du Côté de Chez Swann,* quoted from C.K. Scott Moncrieff's 1922 translation *Swann's Way: Part One.* London: Chatto & Windus.

Qualifications and Curriculum Authority (1998) *Standards at Key Stage 3 – Science. Report on the 1997 National Curriculum Assessments for 14-year-olds: A Report for Headteachers, Heads of Department, Science Teachers and Assessment Coordinators.* London: Qualifications and Curriculum Authority.

Radnor, H., Wilmut, J., Myhill, D. *et al.* (1996) *Evaluation of Key Stage 3 Assessment Arrangements for 1996: Final Report.* Exeter: University of Exeter School of Education.

Ramsden, J. (1998) Mission impossible? Can anything be done about attitudes to science? *International Journal of Science Education,* 20: 125–37.

Reiss, M.J. (1993a) Biology-based investigations for AT1. *Offshoots,* Summer: 4–6.

Reiss, M.J. (1993b) *Science Education for a Pluralist Society.* Buckingham: Open University Press.

Reiss, M.J. (1996) Food, smoking and sex: values in health education, in J.M. Halstead, and M.J. Taylor (eds) *Values in Education and Education in Values.* London: Falmer Press.

Reiss, M.J. (1999) The contribution of science education to personal growth: parental views about science at school. Conference paper, Second International Conference of the European Science Education Research Association, Kiel, 31 August–4 September.

Reiss, M.J. (2000) Science in society or society in science? in P. Warwick and R. Linfield (eds) *Science 3–13: The Past, the Present and Possible Futures.* London: RoutledgeFalmer.

Reiss, M.J. (in press) Teaching science in a multicultural, multifaith society, in J. Sears (ed.) *Issues in the Teaching of Science.* London: Routledge.

Rhedding-Jones, J. (1997) The writing on the wall: doing a feminist post-structural doctorate. *Gender and Education,* 9: 193–206.

Robinson, P. and White, P. (1997) *Participation in Post-compulsory Education.* Brunel University School of Education: Centre for Education and Employment Research.

Rodgers, B. and Pryor, J. (1998) *Divorce and Separation: The Outcomes for Children.* York: Joseph Rowntree Foundation.

Rodriguez, A.J. (1998) What is (should be) researcher's role in terms of agency? A question for the 21st century. *Journal of Research in Science Teaching,* 35: 963–5.

Roth, W.-M. and Lee, S.H. (in preparation) Breaking the spell: science education for a free society, in W.-M. Roth and J. Désautels (eds) *Science Education for/as Socio-political Action.*

Rudduck, J., Wilson, E. and Flutter, J. (1998) *Sustaining Pupils' Commitment to Learning: The Challenge of Year 8: A Report for Lincolnshire LEA.* Cambridge: Homerton College.

Sammons, P., Thomas, S., Mortimore, P. *et al.* (1997) *Forging Links: Effective Schools and Effective Departments.* London: Paul Chapman.

Sandler, J., Dare, C. and Holder, A. (1992) *The Patient and the Analyst: The Basis of the Psychoanalytic Process*, 2nd edn. London: Karnac.

School Curriculum and Assessment Authority (1995) Confidential minutes of the 6 September 1995 KS2 Science Test Review Group.

Shapiro, B. (1994) *What Children Bring to Light: A Constructivist Perspective on Children's Learning in Science*. New York: Teachers College.

Sharp, C., Hutchison, D., Davis, C. and Keys, W. (1996) *The Take-Up of Advanced Mathematics and Science Courses: Summary Report Prepared for the School Curriculum and Assessment Authority*. London: School Curriculum and Assessment Authority.

Silver, R.S. (1998) Dyslexia and the 3D language of clay. *Studio Pottery*, Winter: 42–6.

Solomon, J. (1992) *Getting to Know about Energy – in School and Society*. London: Falmer Press.

Solomon, J. (1994) Towards a notion of home culture: science education in the home. *British Educational Research Journal*, 20: 565–77.

Solomon, J. (1997) Girls' science education: choice, solidarity and culture. *International Journal of Science Education*, 19: 407–17.

Strand, S. (1999) Ethnic group, sex and economic disadvantage: associations with pupils' educational progress from Baseline to the end of Key Stage 1. *British Educational Research Journal*, 25: 179–202.

Summers, M., Kruger, C. and Palacio, D. (1993) *Long Term Impact of a New Approach to Teacher Education for Primary Science*. Oxford: Oxford University Department of Educational Studies and Westminster College.

Sutcliffe, J. (1998) Age weakens thirst for knowledge, *TES*, 22 May: 21.

Suttie, I.D. ([1935]1988) *The Origins of Love and Hate*. London: Free Association Books.

Townend, J. (1994) *Understanding Dyslexia: A Teacher's Perspective*. Staines: The Dyslexia Institute.

Urquhart, I. (1996) You see all blood come out. Popular culture and how boys become men, in M. Hilton (ed.) *Potent Fictions: Children's Literacy and the Challenge of Popular Culture*. London: Routledge.

Vlaeminke, M., McKeon, F., Comber, C. and Harding, J. (1997) *Breaking the Mould: An Assessment of Successful Strategies for Attracting Girls into Science, Engineering and Technology*. London: Department of Trade and Industry.

Wadsworth, M.E.J. (1991) *The Imprint of Time*. Oxford: Oxford University Press.

Welzel, M. and Roth, W.-M. (1998) Do interviews really assess students' knowledge? *International Journal of Science Education*, 20: 25–44.

Woolnough, B.E. (1994) *Effective Science Teaching*. Buckingham: Open University Press.

Woolnough, B.E., Young, D., Gaskell, J. *et al.* (1995) Factors affecting student choice of career in science in Australia, Canada, China, England, Japan and Portugal. Conference paper, Annual Meeting of the National Association for Research in Science Teaching, San Francisco, 22–25 April.

Index